Capitalist Schools

Critical Social Thought

Series editor: Michael W. Apple
Professor of Curriculum and Instruction and of Educational Policy
Studies, University of Wisconsin-Madison

Already published

Capitalist Schools

Explanation and Ethics in Radical Studies of Schooling
DANIEL P. LISTON

Routledge
New York   London

First published in 1988 by

Routledge
an imprint of
Routledge, Chapman & Hall, Inc.
29 West 35th Street
New York, NY 10001

Published in Great Britain by

Routledge
11 New Fetter Lane
London EC4P 4EE

Library of Congress Cataloging-in-Publication Data

Liston, Daniel Patrick.
   Capitalist schools: explanation and ethics in radical studies of schooling/by Daniel P. Liston.
     p.   cm. — (Critical social thought)
   Includes bibliographies and index.
   ISBN 0–415–90044–1
   1. Public schools — Social aspects — United States. 2. Educational sociology — United States. 3. Philosophy, Marxist — United States. 4. Radicalism — United States. I. Title. II. Series.
LC191.4.L56 1988
370. 19'0973—dc19   88–6637

British Library Cataloguing in Publication Data

Liston, Daniel P., *1953–*
   Capitalist schools: explanation and
   ethics in radical studies of schooling.
   —(Critical social thought series).
   1. Schools — Sociological perspectives
   I. Title II. Series
   370.19

ISBN 0–415–90044–1

Table of Contents

Series editor's introduction

The fact that schools do not exist in a vacuum is recognized as nearly a truism today. The curricular, pedagogical, and evaluative policies and practices that dominate education are as controversial as they have ever been and it is widely recognized that schooling is caught up in the social conflicts and pressures of the wider society. The real issue is not whether schools are connected to these conflicts and pressures, but *how* and *why*. Answering these questions requires us to have a more general theory that can explain the relationship between the ways our educational system operates and the political and economic structures of the larger society.

Over the past two decades a particular kind of theory—one influenced by the Marxist and Neo-Marxist tradition—has evolved to try and explain these connections. It has sometimes been more than a little controversial, but it has also made it nearly impossible to think cogently about the role of schooling in our social formation without taking its claims seriously.

It is not to fall back into the trap of reductionism to recognize that in this society, as in all others, there exist general priorities and interests that provide what might be called its historical centre of gravity.[1] We do live in a capitalist society, and that means something to the kind of knowledge that is deemed legitimate to pass on to future generations, to the manner in which teaching goes on in classrooms, to what is ultimately evaluated and the ways we actually do these evaluations, to the overall goals of the school, and to who makes decisions about all of these things. While class dynamics and the economic relations of capitalism do not explain everything of importance to critically minded educators, to ignore their utter import is to cut ourselves off from some of the most insightful tools we possess.

1

Robert Heilbroner has described capitalism as "stratified society in which the accumulation of wealth fulfills two functions: the realization of prestige, with its freight of unconscious sexual and emotional needs, and the expression of power, with its own constellation of unconscious requirements and origins".[2] Prestige, power, and wealth are part of a system, then, that requires some to have them while others do not. This is not actually or even primarily a Marxist point. Adam Smith, surely no Marxist for temporal as well as ideological reasons, put it this way: "Wherever there is a great wealth, there is great inequality. For every rich man, there must be at least five hundred poor, and the affluence of the rich supposes the indigence of the many."[3] The difference here, though, is that the more Marxist-oriented approaches (and there are many, very different, tendencies within this tradition) extend these insights into a set of complex and critical theories of how the economy, government, and culture of a people interact to create such exploitation. Thus, it is not the mere fact of focusing on, say, economic structure that produces severe inequalities that is at issue. It is *how* one does it that counts.

The application of these critical theories to the educational systems of capitalist societies has undergone substantial change and development. This is immediately evident in the difference, for example, between the early and rather economistic and functionalist research of Samuel Bowles and Herbert Gintis and that of the more complicated theories that recognize both the relative autonomy of schooling and the very real power of culture and politics in the later work of Paul Willis, Martin Carnoy and Henry Levin, Henry Giroux, Geoff Whitty, Basil Bernstein, Robert Connell, myself, and others.[4] Add to this the important work that has been done on gender and race,[5] work that overcomes some of the tendency toward class reductionism in the previous critical literature on schooling, and you have an extremely vital and lively tradition that is continuing to become increasingly sophisticated.

Much of this literature is guided by a set of political beliefs concerning the importance of what are called "person rights." In the long struggle between property rights and person rights that lies at the heart of our economy, the individuals within this critical tradition lend their strong support to the extension of person rights, to the extension of democratic principles to all of the institutions in this society.[6] On both the theoretical and practical levels they believe that capitalism has tensions and conflicts—and a "historical center of gravity" —that make it nearly impossible for such democratic norms to prevail.

There is an expanding body of work that supports these claims on an economic, political, and conceptual level. As Andrew Levine, for instance, so convincingly argues, the ideas of democratic socialism (and *both* words are stressed here) fare considerably better than the constellation of principles surrounding capitalism when examined in light of such core concepts as freedom, justice, equality, welfare and efficiency, and democracy and rights.[7]

Other recent commentators have recognized this as well. Bowles and Gintis, in one of the more incisive analyses, put it this way:

> "Democratic capitalism" suggests a set of harmonious and mutually supportive institutions, each promoting a kind of freedom in distinct realms of social life. Yet . . . capitalism and democracy are not complementary systems. Rather they are sharply contrasting rules regulating both the process of human development and the historical evolution of whole societies: the one is characterized by the preeminence of economic privilege based on property rights, the other insists on the priority of liberty and democratic accountability based on the exercise of personal rights.[8]

Unfortunately, while democratic norms and practices are not mere ornaments in societies like our own—after all, there have been long and difficult efforts to establish social policies that support the common good[9] at the expense of greed and private gain—they are actually used sparingly in the day-to-day organization and management of most of our core institutions. In the places where things really get done—in families, armies, factories, offices, banks, schools, and so forth—all too many of the actually existing practices have been anything but democratic.[10]

Yet even given the power of such arguments concerning the contradictory natures of democracy and capitalism, nevertheless the critical tradition in education or anywhere else is immune from criticism. Both the provocative nature of its claims and what I believe is the generally correct nature of its overall position does not mean that it cannot be strengthened measurably at either the empirical or conceptual level. There can be no doubt that the empirical sophistication of Marxist and Neo-Marxist work has grown immensely over the past decade. Similar progress has occurred in its theoretical development. Yet, in order for these theories to be justified in their claim that this tradition does indeed see the world more accurately than the dominant models in education, its practitioners must continue rigorously to scrutinize the theoretical apparatus not only of the dominant model but their own as well. This is what makes *Capitalist Schooling* such an important volume.

As I have argued in much greater detail in *Teachers and Texts*, all people involved in the long and difficult attempt to democratize both the practices and outcomes of educational institutions need to go beyond the tacit belief that analytic, political, and ethical clarity is something of a sideshow or, worse, a tool of dominant interests.[11] A portion of the recent critical work in education has something of a mystical quality surrounding it. Of course, the more dominant rightist discourse in education has had more than its share of writers who are past masters at substituting slogans and ad hominum attacks for serious arguments. But, given the overt aim of democracy, the left has to be very careful not to mystify, not to make its claims in a manner that is nearly impossible to verify or clarify. For mystification has had a number of negative effects: It has led to a partial isolation of this work on the borders of scholarship and public debate, and its marginalization has grown because of the arcane quality that characterizes some of its language. In a field that has historically shunted theoretical work to the sidelines (sometimes for very good reasons, since educational theory has usually involved male academics theorizing about what is largely women's paid labor—i.e., teaching),[12] the nearly mystical quality of some critical work, its tendency not to take sufficient time to clarify its basic concepts or to write clearly, cannot help but limit its impact.

Daniel Liston's project is to increase the possible impact of such work by strengthening its conceptual roots. He engages in a sympathetic but critical analysis of a significant segment of this literature from within the tradition. He is clear on where his political and educational sympathies lie. But this does not prevent him from raising a number of questions about the claims that many educational critics have made about the connections between schooling—and the curricula and teaching found within it—and capitalist relations.

Capitalist Schools focuses on a number of the figures who have contributed to the resurgence of interest in Marxist and Neo-Marxist approaches to the study of education. Among those whose work is interrogated are Anyon, Apple, Freire, Giroux, Hogan, Wexler, Wrigley, Bowles and Gintis, and Carnoy and Levin. The strengths and weaknesses of the kinds of arguments each presents are carefully laid out. This is done not because Liston delights in showing the conceptual gaps and silences within the tradition, but expressly because of Liston's own faith in the ultimate explanatory potential of these kinds of theories *if* they are more rigorously constructed.

As he states it, "Without critical inspections, conceptual frameworks cannot grow in explanatory or persuasive strength." Believing that the critical theories of schooling that have grown over the past two decades "have offered potentially explanatory claims, moral critiques, and practical prescriptions," Liston argues that this does not make such theories faultless. In his words, "I think the tradition can do better." Hence the sympathetic but critical appraisal of Marxist analyses of schooling that this book provides.

Yet it is not only the level of explanation that concerns *Capitalist Schools*. Radical educators don't simply try to explain why the policies and practices of schooling look the way they do in capitalist countries. They also evaluate these policies and practices, often condemning them as being both antithetical to democracy and unjust, especially to people of color, women, the poor, and the working class. Thus, these criticisms are guided by a particular set of moral sensibilities, a range of ethical principles that provide the basis for both the critical appraisals of what exists and the prescriptions for change that follow. Thus, Liston spends a good deal of time examining the ethical justifications that lie behind many of the positions these critics have taken. He compares them to Marx's own theories of the relationship between capitalism and freedom and once more challenges these educators both to come to terms with the ambiguities within this tradition and to build more adequate ethical justifications for their own positions.

Some readers who count themselves among those on the left side of the political and educational spectrum may find themselves

5

uncomfortable with some of Liston's arguments. His stress both on explanations that are more coherent and logically satisfying and on the importance of empirical tests of critical assertions may lead some to conclude that he is simply urging a return to positivist methods and models. I would urge such individuals to read more closely, since Liston's arguments are not at all that simple and are very important to consider if we are to make the case against some of the undemocratic policies and practices of schooling in a more compelling manner. You may find yourself disagreeing with some of his criticisms or with his own approach, but such disagreements and conflicts are at the heart of collective progress.

Those on the right who delight in dismissing radical critics of education will find little solace here in the long run. Liston's efforts are part of a maturing of the critical enterprise. They can help provide some of the necessary conceptual underpinnings that, when complemented by the other more culturally oriented traditions of Neo-Marxist and feminist work, will make critical scholarship even more powerful.

This is not to imply that the ultimate test of Marxist and Neo-Marxist approaches to understanding "capitalist schools" is its logical consistency. These approaches need also to be valued for their capacity to illuminate and pass judgement and for their ability to help move people toward greater understanding of and action on the institutions that daily deny the possibility of a creative and rewarding life for themselves and their children. For all this to occur, the authors of such work need always to be organically linked to social movements striving to build a democratized economy, a democratized polity, and a democratized culture.[13] The increased understanding consistently provided by *Capitalist Schools* will be very useful but of course cannot substitute for such movements. Clearly, there is theoretical *and* practical work to be done. Improving the prospects that person rights will reorganize our institutions needs and deserves both.

Michael W. Apple
The University of Wisconsin, Madison

Preface

Most all educational researchers[1] are committed to understanding and improving schools. In order to achieve these goals, they utilize a variety of disciplinary frameworks and modes of inquiry. From psychology researchers borrow developmental, behavioristic, and cognitive theories, and from sociology they apply a number of theoretical perspectives building on the classical works of Emile Durkheim, Max Weber, and Karl Marx. In the last decade the number of radical and Marxist[2] analyses of schooling has grown. And yet, despite the increased number of radical analyses, relatively few educational researchers think these studies will further our understanding of schools or change them. As a result, many researchers tend to ignore the radical literature. Unfortunately, a number of radical authors aggravate the situation. Radical researchers frequently antagonize each other and their more "mainstream" counterparts, making reasonable assessments of the radical literature difficult. Consequently neither "mainstream" researchers nor radical theorists have systematically appraised the growing body of Marxist studies of schooling.

The possible reasons for this situation need to be outlined. Radicals tend to be suspicious of those who criticize their theories. The impulse to guard and protect the radical tradition is understandable. Knowledgeable of past "red" scares, many radicals want to protect their turf. One unfortunate consequence of acting on this protective impulse is the limitation of the tradition's explanatory power and persuasive strength. Without critical inspections conceptual frameworks cannot grow in explanatory or persuasive strength. When radicals publicly disagree, fissures seem to grow, dividing the radical camp into antagonistic factions. Most members of the radical "academy" are politically passionate individuals, and when passionate individuals utilize a comprehensive and ambiguous framework (like Marxism) to explain and criticize public schools, there are many opportunities for disagreement. Passion combined with ambiguity can create divisive factions. Communication becomes difficult. On the other side of the political spectrum too many educationists tend to dismiss out of hand the potential contribution of Marxist scholarship. For many researchers Marxism is ideologically twisted. Skeptics acquainted with Stalin's pogroms and the failed Russian Revolution see at the core of Marxist theory a fanatical faith and an unyielding revolutionary urge. For others it seems that Marxism's comprehensive scope makes it ripe for numerous objections. Either Marxism's theory of class struggle is incorrect, its materialist bent mistaken, or its political strategy unethical. Depending on whether one talks to partisans of the left or the right, Marxist analyses are either all wrong or all right.

I wrote this book believing that the Marxist framework, and more generally the radical tradition, has something valuable to say about schooling. My goal has been to write neither a radical ideological tract nor a skeptical rebuttal, but rather a rigorous appraisal of recent Marxist theories of schooling. I have approached the Marxist framework as one mode of inquiry among many. My central concerns are conceptual in nature and focus on the explanatory capacity and ethical adequacy of Marxist theories of schooling. These concerns are rooted in the belief that Marxist theories of schooling have offered potentially valuable explanatory claims, moral critiques, and practical prescriptions. I maintain, however, that these cognitive, moral, and practical claims require further critical inspection. Too often radicals offer facile explanatory claims, morally questionable critiques, and dubious prescriptions. I think the tradition can do better. In short, I have written a sympathetic but critical appraisal of Marxist analyses of schooling.

My hope, perhaps unrealistic, is that this work will engage both Marxists and non-Marxists alike. So far this expectation has, for the most part, been fulfilled. While some individuals have read my arguments and found it difficult to overlook the sins of Marxism and others look at my claims and see nothing but a pernicious "positivism," I have had the good fortune to receive critical reactions and suggestions from a number of radical researchers, nonaligned educational philosophers, and others best described as thoughtful colleagues. I am particularly indebted to Michael Apple, Daniel Pekarksy, and Francis Schrag. Mike, Dan, and Fran read the entire manuscript more than once, and they always gave valuable criticisms and encouragement. In the early stages of this project the comments of Michael Olneck and Erik Olin Wright were extremely helpful. Without Erik Wright's encouragement and keen criticism this work would have suffered greatly. In the final stages I was guided by Walter Feinberg and Raymond Callahan, who read and commented on the entire manuscript. Throughout the endeavour I was fortunate to receive both personal and intellectual support (and criticism) from Michael Dale and Wally Ullrich. Without their friendship I could not have completed this project. I am also grateful for comments made on various sections and drafts by William Caspary, Richard Colignon, John Dirx, Sorca O'Connor, Ralph Page, Steven Selden, Louis Smith, and Arthur Wirth. And I want to acknowledge and thank my wife, Michele Seipp, who read and commented on the first and successive drafts of this work. Throughout my work on this project she has been patient, understanding, and supportive. Surprisingly she still loves me.

I also want to thank Judy Stewart and John Pingree for their patience, advice, and labor in typing the various drafts and revisions of the manuscript. In addition to benefiting from the fruits of their labor, I have also been fortunate to receive financial support from two universities and the National Academy of Education. While working on this project, I received an Assigned State Fellowship from University of Wisconsin–Madison's School of Education during the 1983–1984 academic year and a research grant from Washington University (St. Louis) for the summer of 1986. I also received a three-year Spencer Fellowship from the National Academy of Education to support my work from 1986–1989. Of course, I alone am responsible for the contents and arguments in this work.

Finally, I would like to dedicate this work to my son Ira. I hope Ira will come to know human companionship, feel compassion toward others, and have a vision of human community that celebrates the virtues of fellowship, compassion, and freedom. This work represents a small, and rather abstract, attempt to come to grips with why schools do not encourage these values. I hope Ira will come to know and understand more than I.

1

Studying schools and assessing theories

Soon after I arrived at Washington University, Raymond Callahan (a newly found colleague in the Education Department) gave me a copy of one of Charles Beard's letters to George Counts. Professor Callahan felt, I believe, that I might benefit from the letter's message. In that letter Beard cautioned Counts against using the "clichés of communism." He wrote:

Once more, I venture to warn you against your follies. . . . You do exactly the thing which you ought not to do unless you want to be driven very quickly to the soap box. You use the clichés of communism. You in effect call for the abolition of capitalism and point to the perfection of Soviet Russia. In short, you put on a red coat, jump up on on the ramparts and say to the American Legion, the D.A.R. and every school board in America: "Here I am, a grand Red; shoot me." Personally, I think such clichés are damned nonsense and the use of Russia irrelevant to our purposes. American ideals are enough. If not there is no hope. Again, assuming that you are right at bottom, you simply defeat your own purpose. You swiftly prepare the way for the closure of the schools to your writings and influence. Now, mind you, I am not advising you against taking to the streets and the soap box. God may drive you there. I am merely saying that *If* you want to work in the educational world you must avoid clichés, keep out of uniform and work in the historical medium. Subtlety is your only hope for victory with your magazine and your books. Your idea that I should write on "the abolition of private property" betrays the kind of simple thinking that ignores realities and tells the enemy exactly where and whom to shoot at sunrise. Dead mean do not work.[1]

Even though the social and intellectual terrain has changed, Beard's advice seems relevant today. In this decade radical theorists of schooling call for the transformation (not abolition) of capitalism and capitalist schools. Recent theorists no longer ring the clarion bell of revolution but rather analyze schools and society and urge others to transform the world to create greater equality, justice, and freedom. At times the radical literature abounds with clichés, while at other times the analyses seem less platitudinous and more subtle. Nevertheless Beard's cautionary note against using peculiarly red—that is, Marxist—rhetoric, seems relevant. Marxist verbiage continues to raise Americans' hackles; it engenders anxiety and fear.

As a nation Americans have engaged and continue to engage communist countries in lethal battle. In Europe, Asia, Africa, and Latin America the United States has fought the spread of communism. Communist regimes are seen as being directly opposed to the American way of life. Supposedly we fight for American freedom and against communist servility, and we support the "free" market system and condemn communist state control. For moral reasons I can accept critiques of totalitarian Marxist regimes. And as a result of historical and more recent political factors, I recognize that communist clichés carry little persuasive force in the United States. With regard to red rhetoric, Beard's cautionary advice seems sound and applicable today.

However, not all Marxist analysis has been cliché-ridden, dogmatic, or inaccurate, nor need it be. In this work I maintain that the Marxist (or radical) tradition provides a provocative, powerful, and valuable framework for analyzing schools. As an intellectual framework Marxism is capable of illuminating otherwise unexplored aspects of schooling. Recent work in what is called analytical Marxism attempts to present cogent explanations of social phenomena, explanations capable of competing with more standard social-scientific approaches.[2] The authors of these works offer theoretical, empirical, and ethical propositions and they expect a knowledgeable community (both Marxists and skeptics) to assess their arguments. Even those radical writers who argue in a more rhetorical fashion must rely, if their arguments are to be sound, on accurate descriptions and explanations. Frequently, however, the accuracy of their claims is not assessed. Many readers outside of the Marxist tradition react negatively to the evaluative tone of Marxist rhetoric and, as a result, do not examine the radicals' claims. All too often and for all too many individuals, the term "Marxist" connotes a dogmatic and authoritarian intellectual posture. The term frightens people away. Due to a variety of biographical, intellectual, and political factors people tend to dismiss automatically a Marxist analysis. In contrast, those who are already committed to the radical camp tend, when examining radical analyses, to nod their heads in agreement without questioning the theory's descriptive or explanatory accuracy. This situation is unfortunate. When it comes to judgements of the adequacy of any explanations or prescriptions, the color of the framework should not matter. Frequently, Marxist analyses merit further attention. If the propositions are reasonable, then it seems that both the radical and the larger intellectual community should be obliged to examine and assess the radicals' cognitive and ethical claims.

When stripped of its more rhetorical tendencies, the radical tradition offers reasonable propositions. Outside of the educational domain there is a sizable body of radical criticism. When surveying the international situation, individuals within the American left argue that the turmoil in the third world, especially in Latin America, is linked to our exercise of economic freedom at home. National and international corporations support repressive third world regimes in an attempt to keep foreign labor and production costs down. Efforts to create more equitable and democratic institutions are undermined by both United States corporate capital and the United States government. Many on the left have also argued that a central source of our recurrent national economic crisis can be found in the processes and structure of capitalist accumulation. In brief, they maintain that due to the inherent contradictions of capitalist accumulation, economic crises inevitably result. Others have argued that by focusing on the conflict between capitalists and workers the radical framework helps us to understand the transformations that have occurred in the workplace. In part the history of work is the story of capitalists' attempts to organize production in ways that minimize workers' resistance. And finally, recent radical researchers have argued that class, defined in the Marxist terms of the social relations of production, plays an essential role in determining income levels and that the effects of race and gender on income inequality are mediated by an individual's class position. These are all reasonable claims and certainly open to further analysis and assessment.

Plausible and cogent arguments can also be found in the radical educational literature. Central to the radical critique is the argument that our public schools tend to undermine their egalitarian promise. Schools reproduce our unequal society and will continue this disservice as long as the relationship between schooling and capitalism is ignored. The subsidiary claims are numerous. Marxists argue that the capitalist class structure is partly responsible for differences in students' achievements. The structure of public school funding tends to reproduce the inequities of a class society. They argue that the knowledge distributed within schools tends to obstruct rather than facilitate a clear understanding of our social and political world. And they maintain that the differential content and the way in which children of distinct class and ethnic backgrounds are taught add to the injustices of schooling. Rich white children benefit while poor children of color suffer. Marxists also argue that teachers' poor work conditions, their low wages, and their class position contribute to the ever present crisis of public education. In short, neither excellence nor equality can be achieved in capitalist schools. Stated in this manner, Marxist propositions entail both factual and evaluative claims. Marxist analyses of schooling offer explanations, evaluations, and prescriptions for schooling in capitalist societies. These claims seem reasonable, potentially valuable, and worthy of further examination.

The criteria for assessing cognitive and ethical claims do not appear to be that controversial. Minimally, a rational appraisal would expect the explanations to be coherent and warranted by evidence, the evaluations to be clearly stated and substantiated, and the prescriptions to be morally defensible. Too many Marxist writers have not seriously acknowledged these standards, and it remains to be seen whether or not radical researchers can satisfy them. I will argue that those in the radical tradition have not—though they should—pay more heed to these criteria. If radical analyses are going to fulfill their potential promise (and I think they can), they need to be more explanatorily and ethically circumspect. In this chapter I will outline briefly the explanatory and ethical claims of recent Marxist analyses, discuss why an examination of these claims is in order, and identify the obstacles impeding such an examination.

However, before proceeding further I would like to clarify my use of the terms "radical" and "Marxist." I write about a group of radical educators who are informed by Marxist theory. At times I characterize these individuals as "radical" and at other times as "Marxist." The authors to whom I refer are radical in the sense that they believe that the fundamental structure of the capitalist political economy needs to be examined and ultimately changed. They maintain that this capitalist context (and other factors such as racial and gender discrimination) inhibit the realization of individuals' human potential. They are Marxist in the sense that they argue that the capitalist class structure is responsible for a large segment of the inequity and injustice of public schooling. They are neo-Marxist in that they reject the classical Marxist-Leninist call for the dictatorship of a vanguard party; that is, they reject the totalitarian communist state and emphasize the humanism present in Marx's earlier works. Their neo-Marxist orientation is enhanced further by their use of various "recent" intepretations of Marxism. These educational researchers use interpretations of the Marxist framework by people as diverse as Louis Althusser, Gerald A. Cohen, Antonio Gramsci, Jurgen Habermas, Edward P. Thompson, and Erik Olin Wright.[3] While the educational radicals may or may not be personally committed to leftist political tenets (though most are), it is clear that they do write within a tradition of leftist critique, borrowing Marxist concepts and theoretical frameworks. The contemporary educational writers to whom I refer as either radical or Marxist include Michael Apple, Jean Anyon, Samuel Bowles, Martin Carnoy, Robert Everhart, Herbert Gintis, Henry Giroux, David Hogan, Henry Levin, David Livingstone, Philip Wexler, and Paul Willis.[4] For ease of style, I will refer to these individuals as radical or Marxist theorists (or as writers in the radical or Marxist tradition).

15

Schools and capitalism

Marxist analyses maintain that much of what occurs in schools can be explained by the connection between schools and capitalism. At the risk of oversimplification, this connection can be presented in the following manner: schools produce minimally skilled workers for wage labor, and these educational institutions "educate" workers to an ideology of compliance. A capitalist society is marked by class antagonisms among working, professional, and capitalist classes, and schools play an essential role in maintaining these divisions.[5] A capitalist society requires certain general human traits and institutional features, and schools function to fulfill these demands. Basically, the premise is that schools are necessary elements in the reproduction of a capitalist economy. Within the last few years these statements have been the focus of much disagreement. Some argue that this analysis is too deterministic because it does not recognize the relative autonomy schools have in their institutional setting. Currently, many Marxist analyses claim that schools are not determined by the needs of capital. Educators can effect substantial educational change, and schools can play a part in the efforts for social change. However, whether the analysis is one of determination or relative autonomy the empirical claim is that important limitations are placed on schools by virtue of their location in a capitalist society. An accompanying premise is that the Marxist framework can best explain this situation.

Along with these explanatory claims Marxists make moral judgments. Capitalism is a system of wage labor whereby one class dominates and exploits another class. This system of economic and political expropriation is condemned as unjust. When one class, by nature of its position within a structure of socio-economic and political relations, is able to dominate and exploit other people, such a system is viewed as morally pernicious. Another general moral claim brought against capitalist social relations is that they mask the underlying relations. In capitalism the underlying web of supporting relations is mystified, preventing a clear understanding of those relations. Without even analyzing the concepts of domination, exploitation, and mystification and their connection to the notion of justice, it is generally evident that the Marxist framework entails broad moral claims about capitalist society. The educationist operating in this framework maintains that the structure of the larger socio-economic system is unjust and that schools contribute to this system of injustice.

In addition to critiques of public education Marxists make prescriptive claims. Seemingly inspired by Marx's eleventh thesis on Ludwig Feuerbach, in which Marx states that the point is not merely to interpret the world but to change it, a move to construct educational programs exists. Radical theorists prescribe educational programs based on the ethical beliefs found within the Marxist tradition or grounded in the "findings" of Marxist social science.

In short, radical analysts provide explanations, evaluations, and prescriptions for schooling. This admixture of claims is grounded in a very reasonable outlook: The radical tradition maintains that capitalism unduly and severely limits people's freedom, that this restriction affects some more than others, and that such restrictions are easily obscured in a capitalist society. It then becomes the task of the Marxist intellectual to examine and explain why such restrictions occur, to point out that such restrictions and the system that engenders and perpetuates them need not remain, and to indicate alternative futures. At their worst these analyses can be characterized by an undue preoccupation with theory, a confused sense of moral superiority, and a failure to examine the ethical implications of their own educational agendas. At their best these analyses offer potentially powerful explanations of schooling, provocative and attractive ethical judgements, and initially interesting educational programs. In the first half of this work I maintain that the value of Marxist explanations is too limited. In Chapters 2, 3, and 4 I focus on the Marxist explanatory project and argue that those engaged in the recent Marxist debate on schooling have not examined the explanatory adequacy of their functional claims and have neglected crucial empirical investigations. In order to facilitate an assessment of the Marxist explanatory project I examine the logical coherency and empirical assessability of functional explanations in general and provide the conceptual and methodological means to examine a particular functional assertion. In addition to the explanatory emphasis Marxists offer value-laden critiques of and prescriptions for schooling. In Chapters 5 and 6 I maintain that the ethical basis for these critiques and prescriptions requires further inspection. I argue that the value of freedom looms large in the Marxist tradition but that by itself this value of freedom cannot provide the basis for radical educational agendas. In short, I examine the explanatory and ethical adequacy of Marxist theories of schooling.

While many radicals tend to agree that evaluative and pre-scriptive claims should be ethically sound and reasonable, too few explicitly maintain that explanations ought to be logically coherent and empirically assessable. The part of my project that has met the greatest amount of skepticism has been my emphasis on the importance of explanatory adequacy, especially the value of evidential appeals. Supposedly for some radicals (and non-radicals) empirical assessments constitute the stuff of which positivism is made. Researchers, both inside and outside the radical tradition, question the motivation and methodological assumptions behind evidential examinations. Evidential requests are viewed as suspect. Admittedly not all radical writers characterize empirical concerns as positivist. In fact the work of Samuel Bowles and Herbert Gintis and the individual work of David Hogan, David Livingstone, and William Reese are all very empirically focused. Despite the presence of such work, there remains an inordinate skepticism surrounding evidential requests. Therefore, before beginning my examination of the Marxist explanatory schemas, I find it necessary first to address this skeptical audience. There is a strong anti-empirical strand within the radical tradition (and also in the larger educational "research" community). In the remainder of this chapter I focus on issues posed by this skeptical stance and maintain that evidential appeals are reasonable and feasible. Once I address this anti-empirical stance I can then proceed with my more central task, the examination of Marxist explanations and ethical claims. I do not address any parallel skeptical assumptions within the ethical domain. There is no need to. I delay my discussion of ethics and Marxist theories of schooling until Chapters 5 and 6.

Positivism, radicalism, and educational theory

The problems confronting radical theories of schooling include assessing explanations, clarifying the role of values in explanations, and identifying an ethical basis for judgements about past and future educational actions. These problems are not peculiar to the radical tradition. They represent perennial issues in the rational appraisal of educational theories. More recently, these issues have appeared in other non-Marxist educational debates. The noted O'Connor-Hirst debate concerns the value and place of empirical and ethical questions in educational theory.[6] Daniel J. O'Connor maintains that the central task of educational theory is empirical. Ethical and moral questions are not elements in his formulation. Countering O'Connor, Paul Hirst argues that educational theory must include both cognitive and moral claims. The recent spate of philosophically oriented articles appearing in the *Educational Researcher* illustrates further that these issues are central to attempts to study and change schools. Denis C. Phillips argues that when educational writers accuse other researchers of committing errors there must be a way to validate or refute these claims.[7] Eliot Eisner, responding to Phillips, maintains that since there are multiple ways of looking at the world, calls for simple tests of validation misconstrue the entire research endeavor.[8] Jonas Soltis continues the debate, arguing that educational researchers are all members of an associated community and that we therefore need to recognize that

> . . . education and pedagogy have empirical, interpretive
> and normative dimensions; that there now are and can in
> the future be developed ways to make warranted knowledge
> claims in each of these dimensions: and . . . that we should
> open-mindedly presume the good will and intelligence of each
> other as researchers until proven otherwise.[9]

A review of the relevant literature indicates that the radical tradition has not created these epistemological and axiological problems. Anyone attempting a rational assessment of educational research would eventually confront these issues.

While these problems are not peculiar to any particular conceptual framework, there are writers in the radical tradition who have approached these difficulties from a particular orientation. Their response appears to be a result of a rejection of mainstream models of inquiry (frequently characterized as positivist) and a belief in the power of radical concepts. To demonstrate this stance, it will be helpful briefly to describe the radical "critique of positivism" and relate the consequences of these writers' commitment to radical concepts.

In its more extreme and exaggerated form the attack on "positivism" runs something like this.[10] There is present in educational thought and in capitalist society at large a culture of positivism. In educational research this culture of positivism is characterized by a pernicious preoccupation with theory in its explanatory, technical, and predictive role, a corresponding neglect of the role of ethics, and a lack of deliberation over educational ends. Theory becomes preoccupied with means and this preoccupation has pre-empted a concern for ends. In positivist approaches educational theory is myopically focused on "objective" knowledge claims. As Henry Giroux asserts, positivist research sanctions only that knowledge construed as the

> " . . .description and explanation of objectified data, con-
> ceived—a priori—as cases of instances of possible laws."
> Thus, knowledge becomes identified with scientific method-
> ology and its orientation toward self-subsistent facts whose
> law-like connections can be grasped descriptively. Questions
> concerning the social construction of knowledge and the
> constitutive interests behind the selection, organization and
> evaluation of "brute facts" are buried under the assumption
> that knowledge is objective and value-free. . . . Values, then,
> appear as the nemises [*sic*] of "facts," and are viewed at
> best, as interesting, and at worst, as irrational and subjective
> emotional responses.[11]

This critique maintains further that positivism supposes a view of "objectivity" where values are not supposed to taint the search for knowledge. Purportedly the positivist educational researcher practices "value-free" research where "values, judgments and normative-based inquiry are dismissed because they do not admit of either truth or falsity."[12]

In reaction to this "culture of positivism" many radicals assert that facts and values are impossible to separate. They maintain, as Giroux says, that the notion that "theory, facts and inquiry can be objectively determined and used falls prey to a set of values that are both conservative and mystifying in their political orientation."[13] To oppose this conservative orientation, radicals embrace the values of justice and freedom. They utilize the concepts of class, domination, exploitation, and reproduction on behalf of these values. Rather than separate, the radical conjoins facts and values, social theory and commitment. For most radical theorists educational studies is not a neutral endeavour but a political project motivated by an awareness of injustice and domination in public schools and our larger society.

In service of this ethic of justice and freedom and as a reaction against the "positivist" approach radicals began to employ Marxist concepts[14] such as class structure, class struggle, ideology, hegemony, and the State and to refer to causal processes as modes of determination, dialectical relations, and forms of reproduction. Presumably the justification for employing these concepts is that they enable radical theorists to explain how schools operate and illuminate what is wrong with our educational system. Samuel Bowles and Herbert Gintis have presented a correspondence theory linking schools to the needs of a capitalist economy: schools reproduce capitalism.[15] Michael Apple argues that the school curriculum acts as an ideological barrier to a more just world.[16] Jean Anyon claims that students from different economic classes receive qualitatively different knowledge in the public schools.[17] Henry Giroux maintains that student and teacher resistance to school practices is ignored.[18] And Martin Carnoy and Henry Levin argue that schooling cannot be adequately explained unless one views public schools as part of the state in a capitalist society.[19] Radicals advance empirical descriptions and causal claims about schools using concepts borrowed from the Marxist tradition. There is no claim of "value-neutrality." In fact, radicals maintain that traditional researchers have not achieved their reputed neutral stance. Briefly, the argument goes something like this: To accept the predominant research questions and frameworks is to fall into the trap of supporting the powerful and further disenfranchising the powerless; thus, claims of neutrality cannot obscure the traditionalist' support of the dominant orientation. Rather than hide their own orientation, radicals proclaim their commitment. Radicals herald their tradition as ascertaining the ills of schools and capitalism. If "positivism" purportedly separates fact from value, then the radical tradition has wed the two firmly together.

Notwithstanding the radical conjunction of social theory and ethical beliefs, explanations require a degree of evidential warrant and ethical judgments a degree of justification. It is neither positivist nor unreasonable to ask for empirical evidence or ethical justification. Frederick Crews captures part of the problem when he depicts recent trends in social theory:

> The major shift we have witnessed over the past generation [of social theorists] is not a growing taste for big ideas but a growing a priorism—a willingness to settle issues by theoretical decree, without even a pretense of evidential appeal. . . . But today we are surrounded by "theoreticism" — frank recourse to unsubstantiated theory, not just as a tool of investigation but as antiempirical knowledge in its own right.[20]

He adds that "What antipositivism really comes down to is a feeling of nonobligation toward empiricism in the broad sense—that is, toward the community that expects theory to stay at least somewhat responsive to demonstrable findings."[12] For Crews empiricism in the broad sense is simply the "active participation in a community of informed people who care about evidence and who can be counted on for unsparing criticism."[22] Exactly how one goes about gathering this evidence, what counts as a "fact," and the assumptions underlying this evidential search are issues over which debate continues. Despite these disagreements it seems clear that Marxist explanations cannot ignore evidential assessments. In the following discussion I do not resurrect a foundationalist empiricism or a logic of verification. Nor do I believe evidential examination will ultimately establish which theories are closest to *the* truth. I do, however, maintain that any reasonable and useful form of social inquiry must be thoroughly empirical (in Crews' sense of the word). Cogent explanations are those that are constrained by and answerable to a body of evidence.

In addition to Crews' call for evidential examinations I would add a demand for evaluative and prescriptive justifications. All too often radicals are reluctant to fulfill these requests. In the next two sections I examine possible reasons for this reluctance (focusing on the Marxist explanatory project). I do not provide definitive methodological, epistemological, or eithical arguments. Instead I deflect what I view as unreasonable positions and present minimal expectations. In the first section (Science,

Theory, and Evidence) I note that some radicals tend to react negatively to arguments for evidential substantiation. It seems that a concern for methodological procedures treads perilously close to "positivism." I maintain that the radical arguments against evidential examinations are not secure. Another set of problems revolves around the acclaimed fact-value conjunction, and I address these problems in the second section (Theories, Facts, and Values). Radicals tend to fuse empirical and evaluative claims. As a result of this conscious admixture many radicals are suspicious of requests for further reference to "the facts." This apprehension appears to stem from two distinct positions: One view claims that our concepts are determined by our material conditions, our class positions, while a second view asserts that all theoretical frameworks in the social sciences are value-laden. Both positions claim that empirical evidence cannot adequately test theoretical claims. I argue against both views, maintaining that facts do constrain theoretical claims despite value commitments.

Science, theory, and evidence

While the traditional belief seems to support the view that science represents the most rigorous and methodologically circumspect investigation of causal claims, radical theorists have criticized and devalued scientific examinations. These radical skeptics counter with one of three distinct arguments against evidential inspection: one embraces Jurgen Habermas' definition of critical, as opposed to empirical-analytic, theory; another asserts the primacy of a "pragmatic test" of an explanation; and the third argues that standard empirical assessments violate the dialectical character of Marxist theory. I address each argument below.

The first argument is based on Jurgen Habermas' tripartite division of knowledge in his *Knowledge and Human Interests*. Habermas' central claim is that in contemporary society knowledge—all *valued* knowledge—has been reduced to scientific, empirical-analytic knowledge. As a result of this reduction we are left with a pernicious scientism: "Scientism means science's belief in itself; that is, the conviction that we can no longer understand science as one form of knowledge, but rather, must identify knowledge with science.[23] Habermas argues that the empirical-analytic sciences are not the only form of possible knowledge. In his work two other epistemological forms are discussed: the hermeneutic and critical forms. For the purposes here, these three forms of knowledge can be characterized by their method and also by their linkage to a particular cognitive interest.

The empirical-analytic sciences (e.g. the natural sciences and the standard social sciences) incorporate a technical cognitive interest; that is, as Richard Bernstein notes, these sciences are the means by which society and individuals attempt to "control and manipulate their environment in order to survive and preserve themselves."[24] According to Bernstein's characterization,

> . . . the very form of this type of knowledge necessitates the isolation (constitution) of objects and events into dependent and independent variables, and the investigation of regularities among them. This type of knowledge is based on a model of negative feedback in which there can be confirmation and falsification of hypotheses. The search for hypothetical-deductive theories, which permit the deduction of empirical generalizations from lawlike hypotheses, and the requirement of controlled observation and experimentation, indicate "that theories of the empirical sciences disclose reality subject to the constitutive interest in the possible securing and expansion, through information, of feedback-monitored action."[25]

The empirical assessment of knowledge claims is the preserve of the empirical-analytic sciences in their attempt to control and manipulate the environment.

The hermeneutic sciences (e.g., as represented by Peter Berger and Thomas Luckmann's phenomenological sociology and Weber's science of *verstehen* or "understanding")[26] incorporate a cognitive interest of practical understanding. The methodology of this form of knowledge reflects this interest and distinguishes its epistemological stance from that of the empirical-analytic sciences. Habermas writes:

The historical hermeneutic sciences gain knowledge in a
different methodological framework. Here the meaning of
the validity of propositions is not constituted in the frame of
reference of technical control . . . [hermeneutic] theories are
not constructed deductively and experience is not organized
with regard to the success of operations. Access to the
facts is provided by the understanding of meaning, not
observation. The verification of lawlike hypotheses in the
empirical-analytic sciences has its counterpart here in the
interpretation of texts. Thus the rules of hermeneutics
determine the possible meaning of the validity of the
statements of the cultural sciences.[27]

Empirical assessment is inimical to the hermeneutic sciences.
Validity is not based on a proposition's correspondence to an
existing world but rather is grounded in the understanding of the
proposition's meaning.

The critical sciences (Habermas' version of Marxist and psycho-
analytic theory) incorporate an emancipatory interest. Emancipation entails the goal of self-realization through social and political
action. For Habermas, "The methodological framework that
determines the meaning of the validity of critical propositions of
this category is established by the concept of self-reflection. The
latter [self-reflection] releases the subject from dependence on
hypostatized powers. Self-reflection is determined by an emancipatory cognitive interest."[28] The validity of a critical proposition
is determined by its ability to engage its subjects in self-reflection
and to attain for them emancipation. While this brief synopsis does
not do justice to the subtleties of Habermas' argument, as a skeletal
outline it serves my limited purposes. From Habermas' tripartite
division it is possible to draw the inference that judging the truth
or falsity of an empirical statement is the exclusive concern of
the empirical-analytic sciences.[29] Those engaged in hermeneutic
enterprises are concerned with "valid" meanings, and those
working in the critical sciences assess a theory's validity by referring
to its capacity to engage people in acts of emancipation. The
implication is that critical theory excludes empirical assessments
from its purview.

This interpretation is criticized by Raymond Geuss. In *The
Idea of a Critical Theory* Geuss writes that if a "critical theory

is to be cognitive and give us knowledge, it must be the kind of thing that can be true or false, and we would like to know under what conditions it would be falsified and under what conditions confirmed."[30] Geuss argues ably that an adequate test of a critical theory entails more than empirical accuracy but that nevertheless critical theory must be empirically accurate. Geuss reasons that if emancipation through social transformation is the goal, then it must be possible to ascertain that the transition from one type of society (capitalism) to another (socialism) is objectively possible. This entails at least two empirical assessments:

1) that the proposed final state is inherently possible, i.e., that given the present level of development of the forces of production it is possible for society to function and reproduce itself in this proposed state.

2) that it is possible to transform the present state into the proposed state (by means of specified institutional or other changes).[31]

Without the realistic assessments entailed in 1 and 2 above, critical theory would be a utopian fantasy. Geuss adds that some of the methods used in this assessment would be like those employed in empirical social science.[32] Distinguishing these procedures further, Geuss states:

Scientific theories are cognitively acceptable if they are empirically accurate and are confirmed by observation and experiment; critical theories are acceptable if they are empirically accurate and if their "objects," the agents to whom they are addressed, would freely agree to them. A critical theory addressed to the proletariat is confirmed, if its description of the objective situation of the proletariat in society is confirmed by normal observational means, and if the members of the proletariat freely assent to the theory, in particular to the views about freedom and coercion expressed in the theory.[33]

While it is evident from Geuss's analysis that the confirmation of a critical theory entails more than an empirical check, it is also clear that an empirical assessment is a necessary, though not sufficient, step in the confirmation or falsification of a theory. It is this necessary empirical check that some radical analyses of education have tended to ignore.

Other theorists argue against an empirical examination of explanatory claims employing either a pragmatic criterion or an appeal to the dialectical distinctiveness of the Marxist framework. The pragmatic argument states that our theories of the social world change, not because they are refuted by the facts, but as Michael Carter puts it, "because they prove inadequate to solve practical problems."[34] This is not an uncommon criterion for the validity of a theory. However, as an exclusive measure of a theory's accuracy it is bound to encounter obstacles. Just as it is necessary for critical theory empirically to assess the effects of institutions so that the theory does not become a utopian fantasy, a pragmatically oriented test of a theory must initially screen out those theories that are highly impractical. An analogy should be of some help here. Let's say I want to construct a two-wheeled, human-powered vehicle. I might begin with any number of theoretical models of the sort of vehicle I could build. But not all the models would work. The laws of physics and motion do tell me something about the size and shape of the rims (circular not square, thin generally means faster but less traction, and wider means slower but more traction) and the size of the sprockets for my gear ratio. So rather than starting with a theoretical model of a vehicle with square rims and a pedal sprocket measuring six inches in circumference linked to a forty-two inch rear wheel sprocket, I begin with a theoretical model that includes tires with circular rims and a more manageable gear ratio. The ultimate test of my theoretical model is whether or not I can ride my vehicle through the streets. But I must have taken into account certain facts about the physical world in order that my vehicle will have a "riding chance." In a similar vein it would seem only reasonable that before we test out social theories' abilities to solve practical problems, we should examine their empirical accuracy so that they will have a "fighting chance." If we begin with social theories that are incongruent with existing reality, the theories are bound to fail. The most reasonable way to accomplish at least a minimal congruency is to assess the evidence supporting the accuracy of the theory's knowledge claims about the world.

The final argument against the confirmation or disconfirmation of Marxist theories states that the procedures and methodologies of empirical analysis destroy the dialectical formulations inherent in Marxist theory.[35] Linear equations, statistical analysis, and the hypothetico-deductive structure of explanation supposedly violate the principles of Marxist theory construction. Marxist theory does not formulate general laws and then incorporate instances within those laws in order to explain social developments. Instead, proponents argue, Marxist theory identifies tendencies and postulates underlying mechanisms accountable for the observed regularities. Demands for empirical testing are met with one of three responses: Marxists repudiate any attempt to test a theory as bourgeois or positivist; they try to fit formulations into the standard procedures for testing; or they employ methodological procedures that accommodate the distinct character of Marxist formulations.[36] If, as I have argued, an empirical assessment is needed, then the third alternative appears to be the most satisfactory route. It recognizes the particular character of Marxist theory and attempts to assess the Marxist claims about public schools. It seems unwise for theorists to continue criticizing empirical examinations of causal claims as "positivist" or "empiricist." Whether one holds the banner of critical theory, political pragmatism, or dialectical uniqueness, it is essential that knowledge claims be capable of empirical examination.

Theories, facts, and values

One could accept the desirability of empirical examinations but argue nevertheless that such examinations cannot provide critical tests of educational theories. Moral and political values affect our theoretical interpretations and our judgements about the "facts." As Steven Lukes maintains, "Social theories come in overall, though not incommensurable, packages, involving [not only] methodological and epistemological but also moral and political positions, which are therefore also at issue in theoretical disputes.[37] Two distinct positions tend to be conflated in radical discussions about the value-ladenness of theory: One position argues from a materialist position that our views are determined by our social class; the other maintains that concepts about the social world are inextricably wedded to political and moral values.

The materialist thesis

The materialist premise is exemplified in Bertell Ollman's discussion "Is There a Marxist Ethic?" in which he states:

> Marx would not have denied that the statements "This is what exists" and "What exists is good" or "This is what should exist" mark some distinction, but he would not have called it one of fact and value. If we define "fact" as a statement of something known to have happened or knowable, and "value" as that property in anything for which we esteem or condemn it, then he would maintain that in knowing something, certainly in knowing it well, we already esteem or condemn it. As man is a creature of needs and purposes, however much they may vary for different people, it could not be otherwise. Because everything we know (whether in its immediacy or in some extension through conditions and results) bears some relation to our needs and purposes, there is nothing we know toward which we do not have attitudes, either for, against or indifferent.
>   Likewise, our "values" are all attached to what we take to be the "facts," and could not be what they are apart from them. It is not simply that the "facts" affect our "values," and our "values" affect what we take to be the "facts"—both respectable common sense positions—but that, in any given case, each includes the other and is part of what is meant by the other's concept. In these circumstances, to try to split their union into logically distinct halves is to distort their real character.
>   Followers of Marx have always known that what people approve or condemn can only be understood through a deep-going social analysis, particularly of their needs and interests as members of a class.[38]

It seems Ollman is making the following claim: Our class position determines (strongly affects) our values, and our values determine (strongly affect) what we take to be the facts. In this materialist view appraisals of theoretical propositions are influenced more by one's class position than by an appeal to evidence.

However, it does not seem to be the case that social class determines one's values. Members of the working class are marked by a variety of political, moral, and religious beliefs.[39] Further, Ollman's thesis and others like it appear paradoxical and self-defeating. If explanations of schooling depend on the researcher's social position, rational discussion cannot persuade and only power prevails. A central reason for carrying on intellectual discussion, to convince skeptical but reasonable others, is undermined. Skeptics will change their views only when they change class positions.

Instead of Ollman's paradoxical approach, I advocate Israel Scheffler's argument for impartiality. In *Science and Subjectivity* Scheffler supports the norms of rationality and objectivity as ideals that guard against the cognitive relativism entailed in Ollman's position. Scheffler maintains:

> The ideal of objectivity is, indeed, closely tied to the general notion of rationality, which is theoretically applicable to both the cognitive and moral spheres. In both spheres, we honor demands for relevant reasons and acknowledge control by principle. In both, we suppose a commitment to general rules capable of running against one's own wishes in any particular case.[40]

For Scheffler, and in opposition to the materialist premise, reason represents "a firm commitment to impartial principles by which one's own assertions are to be measured and a further commitment to making those principles ever more comprehensive and rigorous."[41] According to him, our commitment to these impartial principles, and not an allegiance to class beliefs, makes possible the shared evaluation of knowledge claims. My own commitment to these principles of impartiality acknowledges that my empirical judgment about education are fallible and should be assessed by others. Now this response to the materialist position does not substantively address many of the central issues. It does, however, call into question the desirability of such a position and points to an alternative route. Scheffler's argument for impartiality is defensible, and as a basis for intellectual discussions it is more pragmatically advantageous. To opt for the materialist route necessitates disavowing the power and goal of reasoned argumentation. A person committed to principles of impartiality can acknowledge moral and political commitments while demanding relevant reasons and justified judgements.

The conceptual thesis

Others have also argued that our choice of conceptual framework (e.g., Marxist versus Weberian) and the framework's implicit value orientation directly affect our knowledge claims. Social-scientific frameworks combine methodological and epistemological as well as moral and political positions. The way we think about social issues, the very nature of conceptual lenses, intermingles theoretical, ethical, and factual claims. One's judgements about the facts are theory dependent and one's theoretical positions are value dependent. As a result, some radicals maintain, one can never decisively test theory through reference to the "facts," through evidential appeal. In short, theories are underdetermined by the facts. I will argue that although the "facts" may not determine the content of a social theory and that although social theories tend to contain implicit or explicit moral positions, neither claim undermines the rationale for empirical evidence. A helpful way to illustrate and examine this issue is to analyze two theoretical interpretations of the role of "class" in educational reform at the turn of the century. Examining Ira Katznelson and Margaret Weir's *Schooling For All* and Paul Peterson's *The Politics of School Reform 1870–1940* will illustrate that two distinct frameworks, while interpreting the "facts" differently, are nevertheless constrained by the evidence.

Katznelson and Weir begin their work with a homily commemorating the egalitarian contributions of the public schools and the working class to our political heritage. They intend their book to be

> . . . a memorial to public education as the guardian and
> cultivator of a democratic and egalitarian political culture
> in the United States. It is also a call to political assertion,
> because social resentments and racial divisions in our present
> commercialized society—one divided by suburban-based

31

social geography into homogeneous polities lacking even
a common political forum—mock the idea of schooling
for all.[42]

They continue:

We examine the history of class and education in the United
States. If our reading of this history is accurate, however, its
telling is of current significance, for the changing relationship
between public schooling and the American working class is
at the root of our current educational and civic afflictions.[43]

In other words, when divisions occur within the working class,
the class that has historically maintained the democratic and
egalitarian nature of our public institutions, our political heritage is
in jeopardy. Katznelson and Weir focus on two central questions:
How has the American working class shaped the development of
public education? How have schools shaped the development of
the working class? Partially, what they found is:

Without a careful consideration of the relationship between
education and the working class in this era [1900-1930] it is
impossible, for instance, to discover variations between cities
in their histories of school reform or to discover why teachers
in some places chose to identify with organized labor and in
others opted to remain aloof from the working class in the
interest of the development of an autonomous professional
persona. In Chicago, for example, where workers in this
period tended to engage in school politics as labor, they
managed to extract many concessions from the business
and professional advocates of reform. But in San Francisco,
where workers utilized their community-based ethnic iden-
tities in battles over school reform, they were unable to win
concessions from the reform coalition.[44]

In this analysis Katznelson and Weir assume a particular historical
terrain. Educational reform during this era occurred within a capitalist society, a society marked by a central antagonism between a
working class and an elite capitalist class. They found that workers
acted sometimes in the interests of labor and at other times in the

interests of their ethnic affiliations, but rarely as members of the working class. That is, workers acted in ways to protect or enhance their position as laborers (e.g., increased wages) and in support of ethnic beliefs, but they did not identify themselves nor act as members of the working class.

In addition, Katznelson and Weir maintain that "because mass participation is fraught with uncertainty for economic and political elites, such elites often seek to develop mechanisms to soften or eliminate the uncertain results of democratization. One typical strategy is the insulation of key areas of decision making from popular pressure."[45] This background assumption enables the authors to formulate a reason for the obstacles confronting the working class and helps the reader to understand why the working class was unable to stem "the dissociation of school administration from municipal politics that diminished the chances workers had to shape their children's schools."[46] When advantageous, the capitalist class diminished the possibility for democratic participation. In the end Katznelson and Weir maintain that because of the workers' inability to organize as workers rather than as labor or along ethnic divisions, they lacked sufficient strength to battle the demise of democratic schooling.

In contrast to Katznelson and Weir's interpretation, Peterson's analysis does not highlight the egalitarian theme nor assume a capitalist terrain. Instead Peterson utilizes Max Weber's tripartite analysis of class, status, and power. For Peterson the history of early twentieth-century school reform is the story of an institution that attempted to secure its autonomy and longevity amidst a pluralistic set of countervailing forces. Class, status, and power are the three major forces that affected educational reform in both San Francisco and Chicago. In Peterson's analysis class does not refer to an individual's location in class relations but instead to one's "access to the market place"[47]—one's ability to purchase goods. Status is the honor accorded to individuals and groups independent of the market standing, and power is the special access individuals have to the state to use it for their own ends. Already it should be evident that Peterson's reading of school reform will be different than Katznelson and Weir's.

In addition to their differing conceptions of class (and related concepts), Peterson maintains the importance of the school as an organizational entity, claiming that "in a society that was economically and socially stratified but politically pluralistic, schools could achieve legitimacy only by separating themselves, as institutions, from particular groups and factions."[48] Using this premise and examining reform in San Francisco and Chicago, Peterson states:

> If external groups were strong enough to establish institutions that could someday rival the "common school," their concerns were given preferential treatment . . . . whenever social groups demonstrated such strong commitments to educational objectives that they began creating institutions that might compete with the "common school," the public school modified its curriculum accordingly.[49]

Whereas Katznelson and Weir put the working class at the heart of their analysis of educational reform in a capitalist society, Peterson places the school and its professional keepers at the center, reacting to the changing forces of class, status, and power.

The different interpretations are not a result of distinct data sets. The two works draw on much of the same primary and secondary resources. Instead, the difference appears to lie in part with the varying conceptual frameworks. Katznelson and Weir assume a capitalist context: Workers are opposed to capitalists and act at times in the interest of labor and at other times in the interest of their ethnic affiliations to alter schools. Peterson views reform as a result of schools' attempt to secure institutional longevity amidst the countervailing forces of income earners, status holders, and power brokers. Their respective historical stories are affected by their conceptual tools. It seems clear that these two frameworks contain distinct epistemological and political positions and that as a result their knowledge claims are conceptually and value relative. With this view in mind some would argue that one cannot assess either theory by its relation to the facts nor compare the relative strengths of either interpretation through evidential appeal. Again Scheffler is helpful. He argues against this relativist view, maintaining that the relativist thesis presents us with a "paradox of categorization." Scheffler describes the paradox in this way:

> If my categories of thought determine what I observe,
> then what I observe provides no independent control over

my thought. On the other hand, if my categories of thought
do not determine what I observe, then what I observe
must be uncategorized, that is to say, formless and non-
descript—hence again incapable of providing any test of my
thought. So in neither case is it possible for observation, be
it what it may, to provide any independent control over my
thought.[50]

With respect to the history of educational reform the paradox
splits this way: If the Marxist (or Weberian) conceptual framework
determines how researchers interpret the historical data, then the
data do not appear to constrain the interpretation; however, if
a conceptual framework is not employed when examining the
historical record, there will be no historical story to tell. In neither
case do the historical data seriously constrain the historical
interpretation.

Scheffler confronts this dilemma in two ways. First he maintains
that categories organize but do not totally determine an interpretation of the data. The Marxist or Weberian conceptual frameworks
sort the data in particular ways but do not dictate the narrative.
Scheffler writes:

> My categories may be said to provide a general determination
> of fresh data: they reflect my advance resolution to individu-
> ate, group, and separate such data along certain lines. They
> do not, however, determine any particular assignment; in
> themselves they do not compel me to choose one hypothesis
> rather than another. My choice of specific hypothesis is thus,
> in particular, not prejudged by my categorization.[51]

Second, Scheffler argues that even within particular category
systems we can produce hypotheses that counter our "most
cherished beliefs." The Marxist can discover that the working class
did not, as a class, press for reforms. The Weberian might find that
class, rather than status or power, was the single most determinate
force for educational reform. In effect, Scheffler argues:

> Observation may be considered as shot through with catego-
> rization, while yet supporting a particular assignment which
> conflicts with our most cherished current hypothesis. It may

be critically independent of such hypothesis while retaining its full categoricity, for categorization is itself . . . independent of any particular assignment of items to categories. We have here a fundamental source of control over the arbitrariness of belief.[52]

Given Scheffler's arguments, one could maintain that in principle neither Katznelson and Weir's nor Peterson's conceptual frameworks need necessarily determine their respective historical stories. Furthermore, within each framework it should be possible to derive interpretations that conflict with the framework's general orientation. In fact, Katznelson and Weir found that 1) the working class did not act as a class but separated into labor and ethnic affiliations, and that 2) the capitalist class was not always colluding. They maintain, however, that without examining the relationship between education and class one cannot understand, in particular, the actions of teachers in school reform or more generally the history of public school reform in San Francisco or Chicago. Peterson, on the other hand, found that the schools' professional keepers reacted to whatever social group could make its presence felt. While Peterson's Weberian framework divides the world into class, status and power, it does not determine Peterson's finding that schools' professional keepers acted as "institutional reactors." In these two examples, and certainly in principle, it seems that conceptual frameworks, even those containing moral and epistemological categories, need not determine empirical claims. The empirical data do constrain what can be said.

While some may accept that categories do not determine theoretical propositions and that such propositions are constrained by evidence, one could still maintain that evidential appeals do not determine which of two competing theories one should accept. Evidential checks may provide a constraint on our theoretical claims but they cannot provide the crucial test between two theories. Social theories combine cognitive, moral, and political positions. A comparison of "competing" social theories (Marxist versus Weberian) would need to compare all of the relevant elements. An appeal to evidence cannot constitute an adequate comparison. I will not enter that debate. I have established all I need to. Minimally, I maintain, any tradition that advances cognitive claims is not relieved of the responsibility to examine the evidential basis for those claims. Regardless of how fact, theories, and values are conjoined, evidential examinations provide a central "source of control over the arbitrariness of belief."

I would like to add that there does not appear to be one best route for evidential assessment. In these methodological matters a pluralist approach seems most appropriate. However, few researchers seem to support a pluralist stance. After the demise of "positivism" philosophers and educational researchers have tended to take one of two approaches to social-scientific methodology: Some individuals have stressed the scientific, while others have highlighted the social in their approach to social science. Those who maintain the scientific emphasis tend to search for a single method shared by both the natural and social sciences and are likely to utilize structural, statistical, and nomothetic explanatory approaches. Those who emphasize the social argue for the uniqueness of social inquiry and move towards constructing a distinct method for the social sciences. They tend to call for more intepretive and hermeneutic approaches. I maintain, along with Paul Roth (in his *Meaning and Methods*),[53] that social inquiry should not utilize a single view of explanation or understanding but rather should accept a plurality of logically coherent and empirically examinable approaches. In this work my emphasis is less on the social and more on the scientific. Given the nature of Marxist functional explanations (my chosen focus) this orientation seems appropriate. However I do not wish to convey, by my present emphasis, that this is the only way to warrant Marxist knowledge claims about schools. Obviously it is not.

On explanation

If the need for empirical assessments of explanatory theories is accepted, then the rather large task of examining the adequacy of Marxist explanations is at hand. This is not an easy exercise simply because of the variety and number of Marxist explanations offered. There are Marxists who employ an Althusserian structuralist framework to explain schools and Marxists who utilize Thompson's historical-culturalist approach.[54] At times it is difficult to know if the explanations offered by these two approaches are competing or compatible; it is difficult to know if the explanations are attempting to explain distinct or similar phenomena. Another problem in assessing Marxist explanations is that researchers cite class as a causal factor but the term's definition and usage varies. At times "class" refers to a non-Marxist category of socio-economic standing, at other times as a location in production relations or even as an active, lived cultural experience. When examining explanations, it is important to know how the concepts are defined, used, and to what they refer. Furthermore, Marxists criticize functionalism but continue to identify the functions of schools in a capitalist society. If schools' functions are identified, is anything explained? If so, what is the form of the explanation? If we are going to examine Marxist explanations, we must understand clearly three features: what is being explained (the object of explanation); how it is being explained (the form of the explanation); and the concepts employed in the explanation (the conceptual framework). Once we are clear about these three aspects of an explanation, we can begin to evaluate empirically the factual claims and compare and contrast alternative explanations.

Alan Garfinkel provides a very useful procedure for clarifying the object, form, and conceptual framework of an explanation. When examining a single explanation or contrasting two or more explanations, we need to identify what is being explained, he says:

> For an explanation to be successful, it must speak to the question at hand, whether explicit or implicit, or else we will have failures of fit. . . . What we need, therefore, is some way of representing what is really getting explained in a given explanation, and what is not. The contrast spaces give us such a representation of one basic way in which an explanation is "context relative."[55]

The procedure of comparing contrast spaces is helpful in gaining a handle on the explanatory objects, forms, and conceptual frameworks employed in the Marxist debates over schools. We can pose questions about the relationship between public schools and capitalist society in various ways, contrasting and emphasizing different aspects of the explanatory project. We can ask:

1) How do the structural features of schools or the individual actors within schools reproduce capitalist social relations?

2) How do public schools reproduce, contingently correspond to, or produce capitalist social relations?

3) How do public schools reproduce the structure of, the culture of, or the individual's place within capitalist social relations?

In question 1 the contrast space exposes conceptually and empirically distinct levels of analysis: Are we attempting to explain schools' reproductive effects as a structural feature of schools or as a result of individual interactions within schools? What are the objects of the explanations, and how do the concepts relate to these objects? Question 2 highlights the type of relationship examined; it begins to orient one to the form of the explanation: Do schools reproduce (functional explanation), contingently correspond to (accidental), or produce (intentional explanation) capitalist social relations? The final question inspects further the object of the explanation: Do schools reproduce an individual's place within capitalism, the culture of capitalism, or the structure of capitalism?

One could use the device of contrast spaces for sheer analytical delight and arrive at a point where all that is left are questions posing useless dilemmas. That would be unfortunate for the comparison of contrast spaces can be illuminating. It not only helps to focus our examination on the object of an explanation but forces an inspection of the concepts employed and the explanatory form. In the next chapter I will highlight these three aspects of recent Marxist explanations of public schools.

In Chapter 2 I examine the explanatory objects, forms, and conceptual frameworks used in the recent Marxist debate about schools, underscoring the problems with the Marxist use of functional analysis as an explanatory form and highlighting the variety of explanatory objects and conceptual frameworks. I maintain that despite their critiques of functionalism, Marxists rely on functional analysis and do so in a manner that tends to ignore evidential assessments. In Chapter 3 I maintain that functional explanation is a feasible but limited form of social-scientific explanation, examining the logic of functional explanation and illustrating that these explanations can be empirically assessed. In Chapter 4 I outline one methodological and conceptual approach to assess empirically a functional assertion about schools, capitalism, and curriculum as well as reformulating a functional assertion so that it allows empirical examination.

In Chapters 5 and 6 the focus shifts from the explanatory to the evaluative features of Marxist theories of schooling. In Chapter 5 I argue that the Marxist critique of schools and capitalism is based on a naturalist ethic of freedom and not, as is commonly thought, on a conception of justice and, to support this claim, I examine recent arguments in the literature on Marxist ethics. In Chapter 6 I analyze the Marxist prescriptive capacity and argue that recent work has ignored the justification of educational prescriptions. As a result of this oversight and due to the nature of a Marxist ethic, I argue, moral issues related to instrumentalism and indoctrination have not received sufficient attention. Finally in the conclusion, Chapter 7, I summarize my arguments, touch on related issues, and outline a way in which the Marxist value for freedom can reasonably affect the Marxist explanatory project.

2
Theoretical debates and explanatory claims

Alan Garfinkel prefaces his *Forms of Explanation* with a single question: "If social science is the answer, what is the question?"[1] Paraphrasing Garfinkel, I think it's fair to ask: If Marxism is the solution, what is the problem? The problem, I believe, is this: Why are public schools as they are? The Marxist answer maintains that public schools are as they are because schools reproduce capitalist society. While this formulation is admittedly simplistic, a degree of purchase on the issue is nevertheless gained. Marxist studies of schooling explain public schools, in large part, as beneficial and necessary for the reproduction of capitalism. As I stressed in the first chapter, in order to assess the knowledge claims of these explanations, one must understand three elements: the object, the conceptual framework, and the form of the explanation. In this chapter, although I will examine all three facets, my primary concern is with the form of explanation, specifically functional explanation.

Functional explanation, and more broadly functionalism, is a highly contested explanatory approach within the social sciences. Whether the discussion focuses on the classical work of Marx or Durkheim or on the more recent work of Talcott Parsons, Robert Merton, or Nicos Poulantzas, commentators have criticized functional analysis as either essentially inadequate or absolutely essential for social theory. Marxists are not alone in their use of functional analysis, and the controversy is not confined to the radical tradition. However, the Marxist use of this mode of analysis is unique and needs to be situated in the broader context of the Marxist framework. Rather than viewing society as an organic whole made up of functionally beneficial parts, Marxists view capitalist society as characterized by a central antagonism between capital and labor. This conflict affects other institutions and segments of society. One result is that certain institutions (e.g., schools) function to smooth over the rifts caused by this central antagonism. In a society riddled with conflict, schools "function" to reduce the strain and thereby maintain and reproduce the capitalist order. As a result, Marxist analyses of schooling tend to highlight the "functions" of schools.

The assertion that schools reproduce and maintain capitalism is essentially a functional claim and constitutes, very roughly, a functional explanation. While Marxists frequently employ functional analyses, they also deplore them. Marxists criticize functional analyses as positivistic, deterministic, and mechanistic, and yet, at the same time they offer functional analyses to explain schools in a capitalist society. Marxists point out the ideological functions of school knowledge, the legitimating effects of ability grouping, and the socializing functions of a competitive educational environment. These same writers, however, criticize functionalism as an inherently conservative and inadequate explanatory approach. A marked ambivalence characterizes the Marxist approach to functional explanations. If the Marxist framework is going to explain features of schooling in a capitalist society and if these explanations are going to be empirically examinable, the confusion over functional analysis needs to be settled.

This ambivalent and confused response is the result of a general muddle that attends discussions of functional analysis. Essential distinctions have been ignored. In order to assess the knowledge claims of Marxist studies of schooling, it is necessary initially to distinguish different types of functional analysis. This exercise in conceptual clarification should resolve some of the ambiguity and ambivalence surrounding functional explanations. A second step is also necessary. In order to understand and evaluate Marxist functional propositions, I outline the recent Marxist debate. In the second part of this chapter I focus on the explanatory forms, objects, and conceptual frameworks of various Marxist theorists. By clarifying distinct types of functional analysis and analyzing the recent Marxist debate, I hope to establish further the need for an examination of proposed explanations.

Functional analysis

Any discussion of functional analysis requires several distinctions. For purposes of clarification I will distinguish among functionalism; functional attribution; facile functional "explanations"; and functional explanations (proper). Whereas functionalism represents a broad set of assumptions, functional attribution, facile functional "explanations," and functional explanations (proper) represent particular types of functional analysis. Briefly, functionalism refers to heuristic frameworks that guide research programs. Functional attribution involves a description of the functions (effects) of public schools. A facile functional "explanation" is a description of the effects of public schools offered with explanatory intent. And finally a functional explanation (proper) claims that an institutional feature or educational practice persists due to its consequences. Among these four types of functional analysis, only functional explanation adequately addresses a "why" question: It is the only one that constitutes a proper explanatory form.

Functionalism, like structuralism, individualism, and scientism, seems to defy consensual definition. Here I will stipulate a not uncommon interpretation:[2] Functionalism is a basic set of underlying assumptions about the social world that guides the questions and explanations of a research program. The character of these background assumptions varies in strength, and I will identify a strong set of theses and a weaker individual thesis.

In *Karl Marx's Theory of History: A Defence* Gerald A. Cohen characterizes functionalism as a strongly committed set of three interrelated theses about the social world. The three theses are:

1) All elements of social life are interconnected. They strongly influence one another and in aggregate form one inseparable whole. (Interconnection Thesis).
2) All elements of social life support or reinforce one another, and hence too the whole society which in aggregate they constitute. (Functional Interconnection Thesis).

3) Each element is as it is because of its contribution to the whole as described in (2). (Explanatory Functional Interconnection Thesis).[3]

Cohen states that 3) entails 2) and that 2) entails 1). All three claims are integral to a strong interpretation of functionalism. Interpreted in this manner, functionalism commits a theorist to a view of society as an integrated whole in which each aspect reinforces the other elements and the entire society, and every event can be explained by its contributions to (effects on) society.

As opposed to this strong paradigm of functionalism, in its weakest form functionalism makes the minimal assumption that social systems exhibit a marked tendency towards self-maintenance. This tendency towards self-maintenance does not commit the theorist to any of the assumptions in the stronger version. The weaker thesis does not entail the assumptions that all elements of social life strongly influence one another or form an inseparable whole, that all elements support and reinforce each other, or that each element is as it is because of its consequences. It assumes neither a harmonious integration nor an antagonistic separation of society. It merely indicates that over time societies tend to reproduce themselves.

Functional attribution is a particular type of functional analysis. A beneficial function (or effect) is attributed to a particular practice or institutional feature. For example, tracking (ability grouping in schools) allegedly has the effect of aiding capital accumulation through the differential training of a future working population. This statement identifies an alleged effect of a particular educational practice, that is, an effect of tracking is to train future workers. Such an identification cannot presume to explain the existence or persistence of tracking; it simply describes an effect of grouping students according to measured ability. This distinction between description and explanation needs to be emphasized. A few examples should help. A function of the nose, for some, is to hold a pair of eyeglasses in place. Citing this function does not explain why the nose is where it is on the human face. Instead, it merely identifies (attributes) a particular function of the nose. Similarly, a description of the effects of tracking cannot, by itself, explain the phenomenon of tracking. Simply noting the effects of tracking (attributing functions) does not constitute an explanation of why tracking persists but instead identifies consequences of tracking.

Frequently, though, the citation of an effect is presented as an explanation. When this occurs, a facile functional "explanation" is proffered, which should be rejected. In these instances the analyst identifies an effect (generally one that is "beneficial" in a given context) of a particular practice and assumes that the practice is "required" (or "necessary"). As noted earlier, tracking supposedly has the effect of differentially training a future labor force, and because it has this positive effect for capitalism, tracking is said to be "required" and therefore "explained." Such requirement explanations (facile functional explanations) rely on assumptions similar to Cohen's strong paradigm of functionalism. Following Cohen's theses, it is assumed that the different aspects of schooling are interconnected with each other and the broader capitalist society and that all the different elements reinforce one another. Furthermore, schools are as they are because they reinforce the larger society. Now if it is assumed that all elements of schooling in a capitalist society reinforce that society and that schools are as they are because of what they contribute to that society, then noting the effects of schools identifies the roles schools play in this complex web of maintenance and reinforcement.

This approach to functional explanation is facile since it assumes precisely that which must be examined. It presumes that educational practices persist because of their effects and takes as problematic only the identification of these effects. Once the effect has been noted, the function attributed, then schools are supposedly "explained." However, once again, the identification of a function does not explain the persistence or existence of a practice, institutional arrangement, or human feature. Any function could be purely coincidental. An effect of the human heart is to make throbbing sounds, and while such sounds facilitate diagnoses, these benefits cannot explain why or how the human heart operates. Schools have an effect of employing bus drivers but their employment does not explain the persistence of schools.

Recently Marxists have identified contradictory requirements: Theorists no longer can assume that schools function solely to maintain a social order, but rather must view schools as maintaining and conflicting with the existing social order. These "explanations" constitute another form of facile functional "explanation." The story is generally as follows. Capitalist societies issue contradictory requirements, and schools are as they are because they get caught amidst these contradictions. Schools must meet both the accumulation and legitimation requirements of a capitalist social order. Sometimes these requirements coincide, while at other times they conflict (contradict). Schools have the effect of training technically skilled and knowledgeable individuals and thus assist capital accumulation. Schools are also said to legitimate capitalism through a seemingly meritocratic system. When these requirements coincide, the effect of schooling is to maintain the social order, and when they contradict, schooling conflicts with the social order. In the late 1960s and early 1970s capitalism was in the throes of crisis. Fewer technically trained individuals were required, and this conflicted with the meritocratic promise that if you strive you'll thrive. Students caught in the midst of this "contradiction" rebelled.

The difficulty with such contradictory requirement explanations is twofold. Like the earlier harmonious requirement explanations, they presume exactly what must be explained. They assume that schools promote or conflict with the social order and that schools are as they are because they promote or conflict with the existing society. A functional explanation cannot assume that schools are as they are because of their effects. Instead, a functional explanation must show that the effects of schools help to explain why and how schools are as they are. If effects play a significant role in the persistence of an educational practice or a feature of schooling, then this must be shown and substantiated. Secondly, these contradictory requirement theories exhibit a remarkable resilience to rejection. If schools do not create effects that maintain a capitalist social order, then it is assumed they create effects that conflict with a capitalist order. At this level it appears that there are no phenomena that cannot be "explained." The citation of an effect in tandem with a requirement, contradictory or not, begs an explanation; it does not provide one.

In contrast to facile functional "explanations," proper functional explanations do not cite effects and then assume that an educational institution or action is therefore explained. Functional explanations identify a particular effect and state explicitly that it is because of the noted effect that a practice or institutional feature persists. Roughly stated, social functional explanatory claims are those statements with the following form: A practice or institutional feature persists *because* of it effects. Biological examples include:

> Birds have hollow bones because hollow bones facilitate flight.[4]
> When attacked, a millipede secretes a liquid sedative because this defense serves to protect its nearby kin.[5]

In sociology examples include:

> A particular set of productive relations exists because it is conducive to the growth of the forces of production.
> Ability tracking persists in schools because such tracking minimizes crises in capitalist societies.

Whereas facile functional "explanations" cite an effect with explanatory intent and assume that the practice (or institutional feature) persists because it is required for its effects, proper functional explanations explicitly hypothesize that an event persist because of its effects. Functional explanations are not committed to any strong form of functionalism but generally do entail the weaker supposition that societies tend toward self-maintenance. In order to assess the adequacy of functional explanatory claims, it must be shown that, in fact, the event does persist because of it effects. Presently I am not concerned with the procedures for testing these claims; that will be addressed in Chapters 3 and 4. Here I wish to distinguish the different types of functional analysis.

Having drawn distinctions between functionalism and three different types of functional analysis, I will outline and assess the recent Marxist debates over education. One of the central goals of this work is to discuss ways to assess Marxist explanatory claims about schools. An analysis of the recent Marxist debate will indicate that there is much confusion surrounding functional analysis (the form of explanation) and that much of the argument is carried on at cross-purposes employing different explanatory objects and conceptual frameworks. By highlighting and analyzing this confusion, the difficulties that surround assessments of Marxist claims can be better understood and an initial basis for such an assessment can be constructed.

The debate

An outline and critique of recent Marxist studies of schools should begin with Samuel Bowles and Herbert Gintis' *Schooling in Capitalist America*. The subsequent radical debate was framed and formed as a reaction to Bowles and Gintis' initial reproduction theses. In *Schooling in Capitalist America* the authors identify two explanatory relations of correspondence and two major mechanisms to account for these relations. Bowles and Gintis maintain that in the United States there has been a correspondence between the historically changing structures of class and public schooling and a correspondence between the social relations of work and education. To explain schooling in capitalist America, Bowles and Gintis examine capitalist America.

The historical correspondence claim states that each major change in the educational structure corresponds to a major transformation in the class structure:

> The three turning points in U.S. educational history which we have identified all correspond to particularly intense periods of struggle around the expansion of capitalist production relations. Thus the decades prior to the Civil War—the era of the common school reform—was a period of labor militancy associated with the rise of the factory system. . . . The Progressive educational movement— beginning at the turn of the present century—grew out of the class conflicts associated with the joint rise of organized labor and corporate capital. At least as much so, Progressive education was a response to the social unrest and dislocation stemming from the integration of rural labor . . . into the burgeoning corporate wage-labor system. . . .
> The recent period of educational change and ferment . . . is, in large measure, a response to the post–World–War–II integration of three major groups into the wage labor system . . . [6]

To explain how this correspondence is accomplished, Bowles and Gintis refer to the power of the capitalist class:[7] "The emerging class structure evolved in accord with these new social relations of production: An ascendant and self–conscious capitalist class came to dominate the political, legal and cultural superstructure of society. The needs of this class were to profoundly shape the evolution of the educational system."[8] When push comes to shove, it is the capitalist class that shoves and pushes.

Bowles and Gintis also identify a correspondence between the social relations of public school and work.

> The educational system helps integrate youth into the economic system, we believe, through a structural corre-spondence between its social relations and those of pro-duction. . . . By attuning young people to a set of social relations similar to those of the work place, schooling attempts to gear the development of personal needs to its requirements.[9]

This correspondence of social relations is achieved through class–differentiated parental expectations, and these expectations are a "reflection" of class experience.

> . . . the consciousness of different occupational strata, derived from their cultural milieu and work experience, is crucial to the maintenance of the correspondences we have described. That working class parents seem to favor stricter educational methods is a reflection of their own work experiences. . . . That professional and self-employed parents prefer a more open atmosphere and a greater emphasis on motivational control is similarly a reflection of their position in the social division of labor.[10]

The noted correspondence between the social relations of school and work and the historical correspondence between class and educational changes constitute the major features of Bowles and Gintis' explanation. Thus far they seem to be presenting intentional explanations for both correspondences; that is, the historical correspondence between class and educational change is said to be the outcome of power struggles won by the capitalist class, and the social relations correspondence appears to be the outcome of parental preferences. It seems that the intentions and actions of class actors "explain" these correspondences. However, when these propositions are placed within the context of Bowles and Gintis' base-superstructure conceptual framework, it becomes evident that they are offering a facile functional explanatory framework. An examination of their implicit use of the base-superstructure model will support this characterization. However, before analyzing their conceptual framework I want to identify Bowles and Gintis' explanatory object.

In one sense their explanatory object is fairly straightforward: Bowles and Gintis examine public schools in a capitalist society. However, as the discussion of contrast spaces in Chapter 1 illustrates, such a broad identification can be misleading. In the historical correspondence Bowles and Gintis focus on structural alterations in schooling and class. They investigate how schools as institutions periodically changed at the local and state levels to accommodate alterations in the class structure, and they examine internal school organization (Lancasterian model, family grouping, and separate group levels), patterns of school governance (decentralized and centralized), and curricular distribution (common curriculum and differentiated curricula). Changes in the organizational structures of schools correspond to specific transformations in the class structure. As capitalism developed from commercial to industrial and then to corporate relations of production, the structure of education changed.

This focus on structure also characterizes Bowles and Gintis' second correspondence. When the authors examine the social relations of work and schools, they focus on the correspondence between the patterning of class–specific social norms and the social norms of the schools. Their explanatory object is the patterning of social relations and not individuals'processes of socialization. Their object is the forces that constrain behavior and not the behavior itself:

> By providing skills, legitimating inequalities in economic positions and facilitating certain types of social intercourse among individuals, U.S. education patterns personal development around the requirements of work. The educational system reproduces the capitalist social division of labor, in part, through a correspondence between its own internal social relations and those of the workplace.[11]

The reader may think I have belabored a relatively insignificant point. However, much of the confusion in the subsequent debate revolves around not only the form of explanation but also the object of explanation. To argue that Bowles and Gintis focus on the structures that constrain behavior and not on the determinate causes of actors' behavior is not an insignificant point.

Bowles and Gintis' use of a version of the Marxist base-superstructure model in their conceptual framework affects their explanatory form. In what has been labeled a reflectionist or determinist interpretation, the economic base (forces and relations of production) determines the superstructural institutions. Bowles and Gintis situate the educational system within the superstructure and argue that public schools reflect the demands of the economic base. This unidirectional model stipulates that the economic base issues specific requirements that are to be fulfilled by the schools. The educational system does not determine the base; it only reflects it. The mechanism cited for Bowles and Gintis' correspondences, the power of the capitalist class or parental preferences, become mere conduits for the requirements of reproducing capitalism. With respect to the social relations correspondence, Bowles and Gintis write:

> The economic system is stable only if the consciousness of the strata and classes which compose it remains compatible with the social relations which characterize it as a mode of production. The perpetuation of the class structure requires that the hierarchical division of labor be reproduced in the consciousness of its participants. The educational system is one of the several reproduction mechanisms through which dominant elites seek to achieve this objective. By providing skills, legitimating inequalities in economic positions, and facilitating certain types of social intercourse among individuals, U.S. education patterns personal development around the requirements of work. The educational system reproduces the capitalist social division of labor, in part, through a correspondence between its own internal social relationships and those of the workplace.[12]

Characterizing their historical correspondence, Bowles and Gintis state, "We have argued that the moving force behind educational change is the contradictory nature of capital accumulation and the reproduction of the capitalist order. Conflicts in the educational sphere often reflect muted or open conflicts in the economic sphere."[13] They note the need to identify the mechanisms through which this correspondence is maintained, but one senses that the identification of mechanisms is a foregone conclusion. In Bowles and Gintis' story the educational system now appears to be part of the "naturally required" order: It all makes sense. Schools are superstructural institutions in a capitalist formation where the economic base rules. Schools, as elements within the superstructure, are as they are because of economic require- ments. If one accepts Bowles and Gintis' base-superstructure model, the central question—why are schools as they are?—is automatically answered: Schools are as they are because of the requirements of a capitalist economy. The only "explanatory" task remaining is the identification of how schools meet these requirements. As noted earlier, such an explanatory framework is facile; it eludes the question through the assumption of requirements.

The debate that followed *Schooling in Capitalist America* could be viewed more as a battle between contending interpretive frameworks than an argument between competing explanatory claims. Truly competing explanatory claims can differ over the form of the explanation and the use of conceptual frameworks, but they must agree on the explanatory object. This debate, however, is characterized by a confusion over explanatory forms, a profu- sion of conceptual frameworks, and a continually changing and expanding explanatory object. The participants in this debate can be organized according to the similarities of response. There are three alternative formulations: the sites and practices approach; the dialectical alternative; and the class-formation approach.

Sites and practices

While there are certainly differences among the proponents of the sites and practices formulation, their similarities are substantial. Here I will discuss Bowles and Gintis' self-criticism and Michael Apple's reformulation, note the respective authors' criticisms of the original reproduction theory, outline, and then assess their proposed alternatives.

In "Contradiction and Reproduction in Educational Theory" Bowles and Gintis criticize their previous work for its implications about the empirical world and political action. In *Schooling in Capitalist America* they argue that the structure of schools changed only when the economic base required it and that then the outcome was always favorable to the capitalist class. Empirically, this limits school change to the demands of economic requirements, so that schooling in capitalist America will remain capitalist and change only when the mode of production is transformed. The political implications are rather apparent: The creation of a humane school setting must await a socialist revolution, and meanwhile political action directed at the internal transformation of schools is a pipe dream, since political action will always fail unless it is accompanied by changes in the mode of production. Dissatisfied with these implications, Bowles and Gintis alter their explanatory object from a focus on structural correspondences between schools and class (and work) to "the dynamic of change internal to the school system."[14] With this altered explanatory object in hand they hope to identify the political avenues that will allow the transformation of schools into more humane settings.

Their dissatisfaction with the outcome of their previous analysis encouraged them to change not only the object of explanation but also their base-superstructure framework. Their former framework depicts schools as totally dependent on the economic base and overlooks the potential for qualitative change.[15] However, their rejection of the base-superstructure model appears to be based not on a disavowal of past correspondences but on a rejection of the automatic nature of the mechanism. Their base-superstructure model assumes that whatever the base required schools fulfilled and that this was accomplished as a result of capitalist class domination. Their altered position asserts that if correspondences are formed, they are achieved as a result of class struggle and not edicts from the base supported by capitalist collusion.[16]

A result of rejecting the base-superstructure formulation is the construction of a new conceptual framework in which "a social formation is not to be viewed as an economic 'base' with a series of social levels successively stacked on top" but rather "society [should] be treated as an ensemble of structurally articulated sites of social practice.[17] Sites and practices are the two central concepts in Bowles and Gintis' new conceptual framework. There are three sites: the state; the family; and the arena of capitalist production. Sites constitute "cohesive area[s] of social life characterized by a specific set of characteristic social relations or structures."[18] Elaborating further, they state:

> . . . the site of capitalist production is characterized by private property in the means of production, market exchange, wage labor and capitalist control of production and investment. The state is characterized by the institutions of liberal democracy and the family site by the structure of power and kinship known as patriarchy.[19]

Within these sites four types of practices occur: appropriative, political, cultural, and distributive. Practices are defined as a particular type of transformative action by an individual, group, or class focused on some aspect of social reality.[20] Appropriative practices transform nature, political practices transform the rules of social relations, cultural practices alter the tools of social discourse, and distributive practices transform the distribution of social goods. Bowles and Gintis summarize, saying that "a social formation is a structural articulation of sites, and a site is a structure articulating the appropriative, political, cultural and the distributive practices occurring within it."[21] They go on to argue that in advanced capitalist social formations these three sites combine to create a "contradictory totality" and that "the dynamics of the whole derive from the contradictory nature of this totality."[22] The dynamics of this totality are a result of the intermingling of sites and practices. One site limits another site (capitalist production limits what can occur in the state site), and practices of one site are employed in another (business practices are used within the state). The mixing of sites and practices produces two dynamic tendencies that have distinct consequences: reproductive and "contradictory" (undermining) effects. An example of a reproductive tendency can be seen where the economic site impinges on education (part of the state) when business management practices are put to use in the schools. This dynamic is reminiscent of the correspondence claims of their previous work. The capitalist site impinges on the schools by limiting the outcomes of what can occur, and schools thereby coincide (correspond) with capital. An example of the undermining tendency is seen when

> . . . the formally equal status of women as citizens, gained early in the Twentieth Century, virtually ensures that the state political mechanisms will come to supply relatively equal education to men and women. Yet the reproduction of hierarchical relations in the capitalist enterprise has depended on the subordination of women to men. The outcome of this discrepancy is either a delegitimation of the educational system or a delegitimation of the economic subordination of women to men in the economy.[23]

Sites and practices intermingle to produce effects that both reproduce and undermine capitalist social relations.

Notwithstanding the new conceptual edifice, their political aspirations, and the rejection of the base-superstructure model, Bowles and Gintis continue to offer a form of functional analysis. When the authors claim that the "requirements for economic success [are] determined within the site of capitalist production [and] structurally delimit the forms of change open to the educational system, whatever the desires of educational reformers,"[24] they have provided a facile functional "explanation." Education systems are, in part, what they are because of the requirements of capitalist production. Although Bowles and Gintis criticize their previous formulations for the assumed success of edicts issued from the economic base, inherent in the reproductive dynamic is just that same assumption.

Bowles and Gintis might claim that given the framework of a contradictory totality, their new schema does not always assume success and therefore is open to empirical refutation. Dynamics are both reproductive and contradictory, and the requirements are either satisfied or frustrated: Success is not always assumed. While success is not presumed for all issued requirements, a researcher standing amidst Bowles and Gintis' regenerated theoretical forest is able to explain anything. If educational phenomena are not required by capitalist production, they undermine capitalist production. The notion of a "complex contradictory totality" creates a framework immune to rejection through empirical testing. Although there is a possibility of falsifying a single assertion, the larger theoretical framework can never be empirically invalidated. A theorist utilizing a view of society as a "complex contradictory totality" has recourse to innumerable ad hoc formulations, formulations provided and sanctioned by the conceptual framework. When a conceptual framework provides such thick armor, its explanatory accuracy is suspect.

Michael Apple's critique of reproduction theory also proclaims a shift in the explanatory object and an alteration of the conceptual framework. He asserts that the explanatory object must be enlarged to include cultural dynamics in addition to structural forces and that the macro-structural focus must be integrated with a micro-individual examination. He proposes a new conceptual framework, arguing that the base-superstructure model is deficient and claims, somewhat ambivalently, that "functionalist" explanations are inadequate. Apple, along with Bowles and Gintis, hopes that such a shift will allow space for political action.

The shift begins with a dissatisfaction over the phenomena examined. The structural account of correspondence relations excludes two important phenomena: culture and the realm of individual action. For Apple and Lois Weiss, "The very notion that the educational system assists in the production of economically and ideologically useful knowledge implies that schools are cultural as well as economic institutions."[25] According to Apple, this culturalist problematic entails an investigation of the micro-level. The important questions include: "How are meanings made?, Whose meanings are they? and What are the ties between these meanings and the economic and cultural reproduction (and contradictory non-reproduction) of sexual, racial and class relations in our society?"[26] Citing Jerome Karabel and Albert H. Halsey, Apple and Weiss insist that the appropriate research agenda must be "one that will connect interpretive studies of schools with structuralist analyses."[27] The role of theory is to uncover the determinants of educational outcomes, and for it to accomplish this task,

> . . . theory has to do two things. Not only does it need to be structural—that is, it must, at the level of theory, be general enough to provide fruitful explanations of how the social order is both organized and controlled so that the differential benefits are largely accounted for—but, at the

same time, it should be specific enough so as to account for the everyday actions, struggles, and experiences of real actors in their day-to-day lives in and out of schools. . . . This requires a particularly sensitive perspective, a combination of what might be called a socioeconomic approach to catch the structural phenomena, and what might be called a cultural program of analysis to catch the routine phenomena. Nothing less than this kind of dual program—one that looks for the series of connections and interpenetrations . . . can overcome the previously noted problems of straightforward base–superstructure models.[28]

Apple and Weiss criticize the base–superstructure formulation for its structural assumptions, its overly socialized view of individuals' actions, and for the limitations it imposes on political action. For them the base–superstructure model portrays a structural account of schools "wholly dependent upon and controlled by the economy."[29] Within this view schools are fundamentally determined institutions. Schools are mere reflections of an economic base, and therefore economic transformation, not political action, is required for programmatic change. Such claims, Apple says, are inaccurate.

The base–superstructure account is also mistaken when it portrays an economic base literally controlling almost every aspect of social and cultural life. According to Apple, the reproduction theory of Bowles and Gintis assumes that everyday actors, like students and teachers, are thoroughly "socialized and do not respond to those determinations, that these people do not creatively act in cultural ways to struggle against the ideological and structural constraints generated by powerful economic and social arrangements."[30]

Finally, Apple criticizes the "functionalist" assumptions present in reproduction theory. First, functionalism points to a set of background assumptions that views society as working "relatively smoothly to maintain a basically unchanging social order."[31] Secondly, and partially as a result of this assumption, functionalist frameworks subsume all of the elements in a society under the requirement of capitalist production. Quoting Richard Johnson approvingly, Apple notes that when prominence is bestowed on the requirements of capitalist production it appears that "nothing else of importance is going on. Struggle, disjunctions, and conflicts are suppressed in the analysis and a model of one-dimensional control is substituted."[32]

In order to remedy these failures, Apple and Weiss construct a conceptual framework that views a social formation as a "complex totality":

> Rather than seeing the economy as determining everything else, with schools having little autonomy, theories of this kind describe social formations as being made up of a complex totality of economic, political, and cultural/ideological practices. Unlike base–superstructure models where superstructural institutions such as schools were seen as wholly dependent upon and controlled by the economy, . . . these three sets of interrelated practices jointly create the conditions of existence for each other. Thus, the cultural sphere, for instance, has "relative autonomy" and has a specific and crucial role in the functioning of the whole.[33]

Focusing on an analysis of ideology, Apple and Weiss construct a conceptual orientation that posits the existence of three spheres: the economic, the cultural, and the political. These spheres are constituted by distinct practices, but their distinguishing characteristics are not presented. Within each of the spheres the "elements or dynamics" of class, race, and gender can be found. Again, Apple and Weiss are not explicit about the relationship between these dynamics and the spheres of practices, but they do offer a few examples:

> The rejection of schooling by many black and brown youths in our urban centers, and the sense of pride that many unmarried minority high-school girls have in their ability to bear a child are the result of complex interconnections among the histories of class, race and gender oppression and struggles at the level of lived culture.[34]

In Apple's account of youths' feelings of rejection and pride are "explained" by the "interconnections" between the dynamics and spheres of practices.

In addition to explanations that illustrate the interconnections within this complex totality, Apple views schools as performing three economic functions: Schools produce effects conducive to the accumulation, legitimation, and production needs of a capitalist economy; that is, schools produce a stratified and socialized work force (accumulation), a sense that the economic and social system is just (legitimation), and technically useful knowledge (production). At times these functions coincide and at other times they conflict, but schools are as they are, at least in part, because of the functions they fulfill.

According to Apple the base-superstructure model in reproduction theory entails a completely socialized view of teachers and students. While in some theorists' hands a base–superstructure model might have such implications, Bowles and Gintis' model highlights a structural account and focuses on the forces constraining behavior, not on the behavior itself. Apple interprets these structural forces as constraining all behavior at all times totally to determine individuals' actions. While Bowles and Gintis do talk of the dominating and subordinating force of the social relations of work and school, these notions speak to limitations on personal development, not to a pervasive and all-powerful process of socialization. Bowles and Gintis argue:

> In any conceivable society, individuals are forced to develop their capacities in one direction or another. The idea of a social system which merely allows people to develop freely according to their "inner natures" is quite unthinkable, since human nature only acquires concrete form through the interaction of the physical world and preestablished social relationships.[35]

They go on to note:

> Our critique, not surprisingly, centers on the structure of jobs. In the U.S. economy work has become a fact of life to which individuals must by and large submit and over which they have no control. Like the weather, work "happens" to people. A liberated, participatory, democratic, and creative alternative can hardly be imagined much less experienced. Work under capitalism is alienated activity.[36]

Bowles and Gintis depict capitalist America as a situation where work relations are neither democratic, participatory, nor liberating. Eventually people "submit" to these production relations: broadly and generally speaking, they have no other choice. However, here submission and subordination do not refer to a pervasive and penetrating process of socialization. Rather, Bowles and Gintis accurately portray the work relations that most people enter. People cannot choose between democratic or non-democratic relations of labor. They cannot opt for participatory decision-making in the office or shop. And they cannot choose a liberating place of employment. They submit to the existing forms of work relations. Within the constraints of work relations people are free to take all sorts of actions, but Bowles and Gintis' argument is that people are not free to choose democratic and liberating jobs.[37]

Although Apple provides a new conceptual framework to overcome the "functionalist" overtones of the base–superstructure model, he maintains that schools perform functions essential to a capitalist society. It seems that Apple's expressed reservations about functional analysis have not inhibited him from identifying schools' economic functions. One might construe Apple's functional analysis as simply descriptive, as functional attributions. However, it appears that his is not a simple catalogue of schools' effects, but an explanation of certain characteristics through citing their beneficial effects for capitalism. As Apple and Weiss say, "We cannot fully understand the way our educational institutions are situated within a larger configuration of economic, cultural and political power unless we attempt to examine the different functions they perform in our unequal social formation."[38] An elaboration of schools' functions provides a basis for understanding schools in a capitalist society. Apple and Weiss do add that

> . . . we cannot assume that educational institutions will always be successful in carrying out the three functions of accumulation, legitimation, and production. These reflect structural pressures on schools, not foregone conclusions. In part, the possibility that education may be unable to carry out what is "required" by these pressures is made even more of a reality by the fact that these functions are often contradictory.[39]

At times schools create effects that meet the economic requirements of capitalist economies, but the schools do not always successfully satisfy these requirements. Furthermore these requirements are at times contradictory: that is, they pressure schools to perform conflicting functions. No longer present are the assumptions that schools automatically fulfill these requirements nor that the requirements harmoniously integrate schools into society. Nevertheless, according to Apple, schools are as they are in part because of capitalist requirements. A facile "explanation" is offered.

Despite the restrictions Apple places on functional analysis, he still offers functional "explanations." Schools do produce effects, and these effects, at times, satisfy economic requirements. The pertinent empirical questions for these Marxist analyses is whether these effects are accidentally produced or whether schools persist because of the effects they engender. The proper functional question is the latter one, and it is a question that requires empirical examination.

The dialectical approach

In recent Marxist analyses, the dialectic has achieved a most prominent place, one reserved for only those concepts worthy of the highest praise, honor, and esteem. For some the dialectic represents an epistemological avenue for true understanding, and for others it stands for an ontological fact of social change through antagonistic forces. Among recent analysts Henry Giroux places the greatest faith in the power of the dialectic. Giroux employs both the notion that the dialectic is a tool for conceptual criticism and that it also captures the process of historical change, and his critique of reproduction theory employs this dual dialectical format. In contrast to Giroux, Martin Carnoy and Henry Levin utilize only the historical dialectic. In order to understand both Giroux's and Carnoy and Levin's critiques, I first focus on Giroux's dual dialectical approach and them examine Carnoy and Levin's analysis.

As an epistemological procedure the dialectic critiques single concepts and theories for their limitations—their one-sidedness.

It also contrasts "opposing" theories and concepts, identifying their corresponding strengths and weaknesses in order to achieve a new synthetic understanding. As Ivan Soll describes Hegel's dialectic, "it repeatedly attempts to argue that categories which are ordinarily thought to be mutually exclusive opposites actually involve each other. Putatively opposed categories are shown to be actually one-sided abstractions from a concrete whole of which each is only a partial aspect."[40] For Giroux the concepts of structure and agency are such putatively opposed categories.

> Furthermore, despite their differences, resistance and repro-
> duction approaches to education share the failure of recycling
> and reproducing the dualism between agency and structure,
> a failure that has plagued educational theory and practice
> for decades. . . . Consequently, neither position provides
> the foundation for a theory of education that links structure
> and institutions to human agency and action in a dialectical
> manner.[41]

In Giroux's framework any adequate theory of education must overcome the "false" separation between social structures and human agency. And it is only within the dialectical interface that the putative opposition between structure and agency can be overcome, transcended. From Giroux's earliest analyses to his current work his dialectical criticism strives to illuminate the one–sidedness of others' theoretical formulations.

In Giroux's writing there is also the second notion of the dialectic. It is the dialectic of existing antagonistic forces. He claims that "class involves a notion of social relations that are in opposition to each other. It refers to the shifting relations of domination and resistance and to capital and its institutions as they constantly regroup and attempt to reconstruct the logic of domination and incorporation."[42] And, he adds, "Gramsci's dialectical formulation of hegemony as an everchanging combination of force and consent provides the basis for analyzing the nature of the State in capitalist society."[43] The empirical world is marked by a dialectic of class conflict and the state exists as a dialectic of an "everchanging combination of force and consent."

With dialectical tools in hand, Giroux judges reproduction theory to be too simplified, overly determinist, reductionistic, and pessimistic. Giroux argues that because Bowles and Gintis link schools directly to forces in the work place, their theory is "too simplified and overdetermined."[44] Bowles and Gintis view the work place as *the* mode of oppression, therefore ignore other forms of determination (e.g., patriarchy),[45] and also "relegate human agency to a passive model of socialization and overemphasize domination."[46] For Giroux the tragic result of all of this is that "by downplaying the importance of human agency and the notion of resistance, reproduction theories offer little hope for challenging and changing the repressive features of schooling."[47] By illuminating a theory's one-sidedness, Giroux's dialectical analysis points to the theory's deficiencies and thereby outlines what further work must be accomplished.

One of the most recent outcomes of Giroux's dialectical analysis is a theory of resistance. As a theoretical formulation its declared value is three-fold: 1) it "celebrates a dialectical notion of human agency . . . and points to the need to understand more thoroughly the complex ways in which people mediate and respond to the connection between their own experiences and structures of domination and constraint"; 2) it recognizes that power is "exercised not only as a mode of domination, but also as an act of resistance"; and 3) it expresses a "hope for radical transformation, an element of transcendence that seems to be missing in radical theories of education."[48] More specifically, Giroux claims that a theory of resistance is guided by a cognitive interest of emancipation. Resistant action is based in a desire for freedom. An analysis of resistance is guided by

> . . . a concern with uncovering the degree to which it highlights, implicitly or explicitly, the need to struggle against domination and submission. In other words, the concept of resistance must have a revealing function that contains a critique of domination and provides theoretical opportunities for self-reflection and struggle in the interest of social and self emancipation.[49]

When the object, conceptual framework, and form of Giroux's dialectical explanation are examined, his theoretical edifice crumbles and his dialectical strategy falters. In short, Giroux's dialectical cant can't. As I noted earlier, Giroux's object of analysis is forever expanding. The dialectical critique points out the always incomplete and one-sided nature of other theoretical frameworks. The problem with this approach is that any explanatory object, worthy and capable of being explained, will be limited and finite. In order to explain educational phenomena, we have to identify a slice, a limited section of our world. It is simply all too easy, and frequently confused, to claim that another theorist's object of explanation is "limited." Giroux's criticism of Nicos Poulantzas illustrates the easy and confused character of his critique. Giroux claims that "Poulantzas's heavy handed notion of the school as merely an ideological state apparatus provides no theoretical space for investigating the emergence and dynamic of student counter-cultures as they develop in the interplay of concrete, antagonistic school relations."[50] Criticizing Poulantzas' "lack of theoretical space" is akin to condemning Marx for not leaving room for Freud. Poulantzas' explanatory object is an entire social formation and its component structural elements. His contrast space is between different social formations and their respective institutional configurations, not between the various internal dynamics of schools in capitalist societies. To indicate that Poulantzas does not leave room to address student counter-cultures does not constitute a criticism; rather, it highlights distinct explanatory objects. Analogously, it seems confused to complain that the mail carrier did not deliver the milk. Giroux does just that.

Another difficulty with Giroux's dialectical strategy is uncovered when we examine his use of resistance. In effect, his theory of resistance fails the dialectic test. He employs resistance in two distinct fashions: For Giroux resistance points to students' behavior in educational institutions and, as such, serves as an object of explanation, while it also serves as a mediating category in the dialectical synthesis of the structure-agency dualism. As an explanatory object resistance corresponds to oppositional acts that are rooted in emancipatory interests. The antithesis of resistance is accommodation and conformity. Following Giroux's prescription for a comprehensive theory, the dialectical strategy should include not only an explanation and investigation of resistant acts but also accommodating and conforming behavior. Giroux only examines acts of resistance and therefore fails his own dialectical criterion of a comprehensive explanation. When resistance is employed as a mediating category, the concept of resistance purportedly resolves the structure-agency opposition. However, and again impelled by the dialectical approach, the concept of resistance has its conceptual antithesis–accommodation. Giroux chooses not to mediate these two oppositional categories with a third concept, but instead stops with resistance. The dialectic seems arbitrarily curtailed.

Giroux would probably claim that the emphasis on resistance, both conceptually and as an explanatory object, is due to it "critical function," its potential for emancipatory action. As a form of explanation, the dialectic is valid only to the degree that it encourages liberating action. However, as I argued in the introductory chapter (following Raymond Geuss), any critical theory that aims at emancipatory action must make cognitive assessments that are empirically accurate. An exclusive focus on resistance, neglecting accommodation, is bound to foil the best–laid emancipatory plans. If social action is motivated by emancipatory interests, it is also curtailed by dependency and habit. An account of one without the other would appear to be empirically incorrect and practically insufficient.

Giroux is not unconcerned with empirical accuracy. Although he criticizes Bowles and Gintis' reproduction theory for its lack of comprehensiveness, he states that "there is enough evidence to support that [Bowles and Gintis'] view."[51] Giroux claims that Bowles and Gintis' functional analysis is true and supported by evidence. While I must leave the empirical examination of Giroux's dialectical explanations to others, I want to determine how to assess functional explanations. Giroux does not tell us how he came by that assessment, and that is what we need to know.

Whereas Giroux utilizes both the epistemological and onotological forms of dialectical analysis, Carnoy and Levin employ only the latter approach stressing the existence of "contradictory" dynamics. They criticize Bowles and Gintis (and their own earlier works)[52] as functionalist, that is, as inadequate explanations of school and work. They offer instead a dialectical conceptual framework. For Carnoy and Levin the explanatory object, the relationship between education and work, is characterized by a dialectic. The relationship is "composed of a perpetual tension between two dynamics, the imperatives of capitalism and those of democracy in all its forms."[53] Schools serve two contradictory purposes: They meet the requirements of an unequal capitalist economy, and they serve the demands of an egalitarian democratic state. The opposing pulls, the tensions created by this dialectic, explain the relationship between schools and work.

According to Carnoy and Levin, in functionalist accounts "institutions can be understood only in terms of how they serve society."[54] In functionalist frameworks schools are examined in light of how they adjust students to their future work lives. Carnoy and Levin maintain that *critical* functionalist accounts (e.g., Bowles and Gintis') are valuable for they tell us how the fit between schools and work is actually achieved. Purportedly Bowles and Gintis show how schooling turns students against one another through competitive studies, how students are motivated to work for extrinsic rather than intrinsic rewards, and how schools legitimate work relations and societal norms.[55] However, Carnoy and Levin argue, such explanations are incomplete and therefore inadequate. Bowles and Gintis do not "account for the contradictory trends toward equality and democracy in education. . . . Indeed, Bowles and Gintis argue that the 'laws and motion' of correspondence are so dominant that democratic or egalitarian reforms must necessarily fail or be limited in their impact."[56] In short, Carnoy and Levin state that Bowles and Gintis cannot "adequately explain the relationship between education and work."[57]

Carnoy and Levin maintain not only that the relationship between education and work is more complex than Bowles and Gintis allow but that the relationship is contradictory. Schools are not simply the product of the dynamics of capitalism, nor do schools simply meet capital's needs. Schools are also an "arena of social conflict," part of the democratic state that attempts to adjudicate the inequities resulting from capitalism. Schools appear to have two functions: (1) education's "role then is seen as improving the social position of have-not groups by making relevant knowledge and certification available to them," and (2) schools must "by their very nature" reproduce capitalist relations of production.[58]

Schools' egalitarian and inegalitarian dynamics are, in Carnoy and Levin's historical account, the result of class actors struggling in both the political and economic realms of society. They argue that in the earlier part of this century

. . . employers and professional educators shaped the organization and curriculum of schools to meet the needs of developing capitalism. They pushed for the tracking of students in high schools and the hierarchical development of secondary education in conjunction with segmented labor markets. But at the same time, the educational system expanded rapidly to incorporate the demands on the part of the parents for greater access to public secondary schooling for their children. By the 1920s and the 1930s secondary education was considered a right by most American families. As the curriculum and tracking system were being shaped to accommodate a segmented labor-market system, educators were pressured even more to open up secondary education to working-class families desiring social mobility for their children.[59]

According to Carnoy and Levin, schools serve contradictory purposes, and these purposes are achieved through the class actions of employers, professional educators, and the working class.

Despite the "contradictory tendencies" in their dialectical framework, Carnoy and Levin offer a facile functional "explanation." In their conceptual framework schools are viewed as reacting to the pressures of contradictory forces: the egalitarian needs of the democratic state and the unequal drives of a capitalist wage–labour system. Carnoy and Levin do posit class actors and class struggle as elements in their dialectical analysis, but as in Bowles and Gintis', in Carnoy and Levin's argument these actors appear to function as mere conduits for the contradictory requirements of capital and the democratic state. Carnoy and Levin assume that the contradictory requirements exist and that schools are as they are because of these conflicting claims. Notwithstanding this claim of contradictory dynamics, Carnoy and Levin come awfully close to claiming that schools function to meet the economic requirements of capitalism:

Schooling expands in response to subordinate-group demands, but as long as the class–race–gender structures are the underlying attributes of the society, only the form but not the substance of the reproductive role of schooling

will change. Thus, the class-reproductive curriculum becomes
more "hidden" when there are working-class demands, when
the states are required to equalize access to education for
blacks and Hispanics, or when schools alter the advising
of young women so that they are not counseled out
of sciences and mathematics. As we have shown,
however, administrators, teachers, and parents still tend to
reproduce capitalist relations of production and the division
of knowledge associated with segmented–labor–market
occupational roles.[60]

Regardless of assertions about contradictions and the dialectic,
Carnoy and Levin offer a facile functional "explanation": schools
function to reproduce capitalism. If schools are to be explained
by their consequences, then it must be shown that educational
practices persist because of the consequences they produce. It
needs to be empirically ascertained that certain educational
practices are selected and persist due to their positive effects
for capitalism. Carnoy and Levin assert that this is the case, but
they have not shown how this occurs. Furthermore, if we accept
their dialectical conceptual framework it seems that with dialectic
in hand they can "capably" explain most everything. If schools do
not create effects that maintain capitalism, then schools serve an
egalitarian dynamic. It is difficult to assess empirically theories with
such dense and resilient explanatory armor.

The class–formation approach

Whereas Bowles and Gintis, Apple and Weiss, Giroux, and
Carnoy and Levin criticise but ultimately accept (in one form
or another) functional analyses of schools, the class–formation
framework ostensibly rejects all types of functional analysis. The
class–formation approach entails a radical shift in the form and
object of explanation. Rather than focusing on schools' effects in
a capitalist society authors such as David Hogan, Philip Wexler,
and Paul Willis want to explain, in Wexler's words, "society as
the practical material accomplishment of conflicting groups of
collective actors struggling for control of the field of historic

cultural action."[61] Their explanatory object is class formation and the transformation of schools, and they employ intentional, not functional, explanations.[62] Whereas a functional explanation claims that the persistence of an institutional feature is explained by its effects, an intentional explanation claims that the institutional feature is explained by the intentions and actions of social actors. This distinction is crucial for the class–formation approach. Functional explanation highlights effects to explain phenomena while intentional explanation points to people's purposeful actions. Since these authors' explanatory object concerns the formation of classes and how this formation affects students' education and schools, they utilize intentional explanations. These radical researchers want to examine the choices people make and the effects of their choices as they struggle to achieve their educational objectives in a capitalist society.

The class-formation critique of reproduction theory highlights its "functionalist" assumptions. While claiming to reject all types of functional analysis, this approach essentially critiques the strong paradigm of functionalism and facile functional "explanations." The authors argue that descriptions of effects do not constitute explanations, that functional assertions are tautological, and that functional analysis implies a reified and static view of the world. Supporting his argument against functional analysis, Hogan states that

> . . . although it is obvious that schooling plays certain roles or functions for capitalism, this emphatically is not to claim that schooling in capitalist societies can be explained in "functionalist" terms. It is all too easy as Katznelson suggests "to confuse the difference between the claim that capitalism and schooling have a functional relationship with the claim that schooling was the required institution to perform a given function for the reproduction of the system." The relationship between a particular structure of schooling and a particular structure of capitalism is irreducibly contingent, the outcome of complete conflicts and choices, not of some functionalist imperatives.[63]

Essentially, Hogan is asserting that the citation of functional imperatives (requirements) has no explanatory value. The history of schooling in capitalist America can only be explained as the result of social conflict and individual choices.

Willis argues that the reproduction account simply tells us in rather abstract language what must be accepted as common sense truth.

> It indicates that, despite confusing ambitions to the contrary in the Educational sphere, a social relationship is continuously achieved for the purpose of the continuance of Capital formation. But in a certain way this is tautologous—we know from the evidence of our eyes that Capitalism continues and that most kids go to school. Ergo schools are implicated in the formation of the social relationship which is a condition for the functioning of capitalism. For an explanatory account which avoids this formalism and rationalism, we need a notion of the actual formation of classes—in relationship to each other to be sure—but which nevertheless have their own profane material existence . . .[64]

Again, Willis, like Hogan, counterposes facile functional "explanations" and intentional explanations of class formation.

Wexler argues that the proponents of reproduction theory are dupes of the ruling class.

> Apple following Hall, claims that reproduction theory is not functionalist because reproduction occurs, in part, through contestation and because the society which is produced contains hierarchy. What they both miss is that functionalism is a way of thinking that accepts the ruling group's social victories and pronouncements of its hegemony as social order. It accomplishes that acceptance by reifying and naturalizing collective history as systems operations.[65]

According to Wexler, functionalist approaches view class as a "static relational attribute" and not as a "historical process of group formation in social antagonism."[66]

All three of these authors highlight the defects of facile functional "explanations" or the strong paradigm of functionalism and offer intentional explanations as the necessary antidote. Hogan's historical agenda examines the avenues open to working–class families in the early part of this century and the choices they made. Working–class educational outcomes are not predetermined by capitalist ideological mystification or strict economic requirements. Instead these educational outcomes are the product of working–class efforts, a peculiar cultural production, through which they attempt to control their own lives. Hogan has found that in the working–class members' attempt to control their own lives, "they harnessed themselves to the dominant structures of liberal capitalist society."[67] Despite their differences the various proponents of the class–formation approach all focus on the cultural production of the working class. They are not directly concerned with explaining the structures that impinge on action but the action itself. For some it is through studying the choices of class agents that class opposition, rather than functional harmony, can be uncovered.[68] For others it is through an examination of cultural production that a view of abstract functional requirements can be dissolved and in its place an account of the "ironic and paradoxical" working–class formation can be gleaned. Whatever the motivation, their announced explanatory object is the process of class formation. In order to explain this phenomenon, they reject functional assertions and instead examine the choices actors make in historical contexts.

While all of the class–formation proponents are critical of functional assertions, the temptation to make facile functional "explanations" still exists. Hogan "explains" the predominance of status attainment studies and the focus on issues of inequality in educational research by citing the requirements of capitalism. According to him, "The reasons for the dominance of the inequality problematic are grounded in the legitimation and social policy needs of liberal capitalism, generating a research tradition that Habermas describes as 'rational–technical' or 'empirical–analytic.' "[69] Indeed, it seems odd to condemn and then utilize facile functional "explanations." Whatever the reasoning may be, it appears that even within the class–formation approach confusion about functional explanations exists.

If the class–formation research agenda is concerned with analyzing the processes through which classes and groups form and act around educational issues, it must be acknowledged that their explanatory object is distinct from that of functional explanation. Given the nature of their explanatory object, they would be ill–advised to employ a functional form of explanation. Their concern is not with how the effects of an educational action or institutional feature contribute to an explanation of its (the action's or feature's) persistence but rather the outcomes of individual and group behavior.

Conclusion

In spite of the debates surrounding reproduction theory the original problems still remain. If radicals insist on explaining educational events through a citation of their effects, how are we to assess these explanations? Educational Marxists, while critical of a strong paradigm of functionalism, employ facile functional "explanations" that either assume the truth of their propositions or are framed in a manner immune to empirical examination. Knowledge claims are made about the educational world, and yet the procedures to assess these claims are nowhere discussed. Instead, the arguments surrounding reproduction theory can be characterized as theoretical battles that continually alter the explanatory object and the conceptual framework while using confused, if not illicit, forms of explanation.

Two other interpretations of this debate should be considered briefly. First, perhaps each noted functional formulation should be construed as simply a broad and high–level generalization, one that is, as Katznelson and Weir say, "no more, but also no less, than a plausible statement about social reality."[70] As such these functional statements could be seen as initial formulations describing the relationship between schooling and capitalism and could be treated as opportunities "to develop explanations of how these connections might actually work."[71] Construed in this manner, functional claims would represent descriptions, not explanations. They would note relationships among institutions, practices, and their effects. When viewed in this light, these functional "descriptions" would be exactly like the category of functional attribution. In functional attributions beneficial effects (or functions) are attributed to particular practices or institutional features, and a description is offered. However, many functional propositions cannot be accurately portrayed in this manner. Most of the authors I've examined endow functional claims with explanatory and causal significance. They appear to be indicating not simply that schools produce particular effects but that these educational practices persist because of the effects they produce. When functional propositions are accorded such explanatory weight, it would seem ill–advised to construe them simply as descriptions. When it is argued that schools are as they are because of the consequences they produce, then it must be shown how these consequences contribute to the persistence of the educational practices in question.

A second intepretation is possible. According to this second stance, I expect too much from these various theoretical frameworks. Bowles and Gintis, Apple and Weiss, Giroux, and Carnoy and Levin provide very general theoretical frameworks, not bona fide explanations. Their theories, if adequate, should enable further examinations of schools and capitalism and highlight otherwise unobserved aspects of schooling. If they generate useful and illuminating hypotheses, then they are probably good theories. Simply because the theories, at this general level, cannot be empirically assessed does not mean that they are inadequate. In line with Imre Lakatos' view of scientific theories,[72] our concern should be with whether these theories can support progressive research programs. If they can, then they are indeed adequate.

As a general formulation of what constitutes a research program this account seems plausible. However, I think such an account cannot readily be imposed on these theorists' works. It seems clear to me that many of the authors examined in this chapter portend to offer adequate explanations and that their works are received as explanatory statements. My analysis is intended to have shown that these theories rely on weak functional claims. If we are to consider these works as general formulations—as initial elaborations of research programs rather than as attempts at adequate explanations—then I can safely suggest that the criticisms presented in this chapter guide and inform future explanatory attempts. Specifically, if Marxist analysts wish to pursue functional explanations, it seems clear they should 1) reduce their reliance on functionalist assumptions, 2) formulate researchable functional propositions, and 3) assess the empirical basis for their properly formulated functional claims.

In order to assess Marxist functional claims, the explanatory form has to be transformed from a facile functional "explanation" to a proper functional explanation. Once this is achieved, procedures can be constructed to examine the evidence. However, this agenda assumes that what I have called proper functional explanations constitute an adequate explanatory form. Given the existing doubts surrounding functional explanations, this claim must be substantiated. That will be the topic of the next chapter.

3
The logic and assessment of functional explanations

Recent Marxist analyses of education can be characterized by an ambivalence toward and confusion over functional explanation. It seems unwarranted and illicit functional assertions are more common than warranted claims. But if functional propositions are going to be accorded explanatory status, they need to be logically coherent and empirically assessable. And if Marxism is going to represent a viable conceptual framework, one capable of explaining aspects of schooling, then this situation requires further attention. The problems in functional analysis cannot be solved by references to previous philosophical analyses or settled arguments in social theory since functional explanation, and more broadly teleological analyses, have been and continue to be highly contested explanatory forms.[1] Here I cannot begin to address all of the questions surrounding the specific topic of functional explanation, much less the difficulties attending the more general discussion of teleological analysis. However, since I asserted in Chapter 2 that functional explanation can constitute an adequate explanatory form and since there is a confusion over and reliance on functional analysis, certain critical issues should be addressed.

Numerous Marxist and non-Marxist critics have objected to functional explanation. Radical critics argue that functional explanations assume societal norms of cohesion and harmony and exclude accounts of conflict and resistance. In a more formal vein Marxists and non-Marxists alike argue that functional explanations entail confused causal claims. They maintain that since functional explanations cite effects to account for the persistence of a practice, an effect is mistakenly accorded causal strength. Effects occur after causes; effects cannot be causes. To claim otherwise, to countenance effects as causes, entails a specious account of "backward" causation. In addition to these criticisms others argue that functional explanations are tautological propositions and as such do not "require" evidential substantiation. In this chapter I address these criticisms. I examine the arguments which maintain that functional explanations 1) exclude accounts of resistance, conflict, and contradiction and therefore cannot sustain a Marxist analysis, 2) entail an illicit backward causation and therefore are formally irreparable, and 3) are tautological and therefore empirically irrefutable.

The analysis unfolds as follows. Initially I think it is helpful to outline, in a rudimentary fashion, a plausible interpretation of functional explanations. The logic of functional explanations is not straightforward and, in fact, some critics would say that the meaning of these explanatory claims defies reasonable interpretation. In the first section (The meaning of functional explanation) I emphasize the importance of the notions of a dispositional fact and contextual selection for an understanding of functional explanation, a basic elaboration that should resolve any initial perplexity. In the second section (Functional explanations and conflict) I address partially the criticisms that functional explanations exclude accounts of conflict. This discussion deflects what I consider to be unreasonable appraisals and prepares the way for a later consideration of a more discerning critique. (I return to the "conflict criticism" in the final section of this chapter.) In the third section (Cohen's defense of functional explanation) I outline Gerald A. Cohen's argument concerning the form and explanatory adequacy of functional explanations. On this basis, the charge of illicit backward causation is answered directly. A response to the criticism of empirical irrefutability constitutes the remainder of this chapter. In the fourth section (Testing functional explanations) I outline and criticize Cohen's suggested procedure for testing functional explanations, while in section five (Functional explanations and selective mechanisms) I argue for the need to cite mechanisms in order adequately to assess these explanations. And finally in the sixth section (Mechanisms of social selection) I discuss the types of mechanisms appropriate to an investigation of social phenomena. In this manner I present functional explanation as a defensible, but limited, form of explanation.

A caveat is in order before commencing. Throughout this chapter I talk of "testing" and examining the adequacy of explanations. I also draw analogies between precedence ("normal" causal) laws and consequences (functional) laws.[2] In recent "critical theoretical" analyses such terminology raises the specter of "positivism." Explanations that point to causal regularities and focus on finite aspects of reality are characterized as either "positivist" or "magical" and are therefore impugned.[3] As I argued earlier (see Chapter 1) such charges are questionable. They all too frequently assume one model of science, one model of explanation, and, in effect, one way of warranting knowledge claims. I take it as given that distinct philosophical models of science and explanation exist and assume that a realist account (as distinguished from a positivist or instrumentalist approach) is the most philosophically defensible and empirically accurate account of science. I cannot argue that here. It would take us too far afield.[4] However, I do wish to relate a central distinction between positivist and realist accounts of explanation, for, as this chapter unfolds, I employ Cohen's account of explanation, essentially a deductive–nomological model, to clarify and analyze an account of functional explanation. In short, I temporarily utilize what some have called a "positivist" model of explanation in order eventually to support and elaborate my own account. My goal, and the outcome of my analysis, is a form of explanation that is characteristically realist rather than "positivist." I've chosen this route for expository purposes. Such an analysis is attractive, I believe, both for its persuasiveness and clarity.

Briefly, the deductive–nomological (D–N) structure of explanation is as follows.[5] In the D–N model an institutional feature (social practice or event) is explained if it can be logically subsumed under pertinent general laws and appropriate antecedent conditions. The structure of this type of explanation consists of two basic components: an explanans (the premise) and the explanandum (the conclusion). The explanans consists of statements of general laws and instances of particular conditions. The explanandum is the "fact," the educational practice or institutional feature, to be explained. In the D–N model the explanandum is deduced from the general laws and the antecedent conditions. Graphically, the structure can be formulated in the following manner:

Explanans: General Laws $(L_1, L_2, L_3, \ldots L_n)$
(Premise)   Antecedent Conditions $(C_1, C_2, C_3, \ldots C_n)$

Explanandum: Educational Practice
(Conclusion)

Substantively, this model can be illustrated through the following example. In order to explain the increased learning occurring in one classroom, one might be able to subsume that event under a few pertinent general laws and antecedent conditions. One of the general laws might state: Whenever students increase "time on task," learning is enhanced. And one of the antecedent conditions might be that the students did, in fact, spend more time on task. Using a D–N model the investigator could conclude that the increased learning (the conclusion) follows logically from the noted time on task regularity and the actual increased student time on educational tasks (the premise). The enhanced learning in that particular class would be explained.

The realist criticizes this approach, arguing that it is unable to provide an adequate causal account. While a regular relationship (increased time on task results in greater learning) enables future prediction, it does not explain *why* this regularity occurs. The realist argues that two distinct assumptions underlie this confounding of expectation with explanation: 1) a reliance on logical relations and 2) a Humean conception of causality. Rather than viewing explanations largely as relations of logical entailment, the realist attempts to explain an event through the inspection of causal connections, linking cause and effect. While the realist would agree that logical inference may be integral to explanation, alone it is insufficient. Natural and social mechanisms, not logical connections, form the backbone of the realist causal account. In the D–N model the reliance on logical entailment (and the corresponding inattention to mechanisms) is reinforced by traditional Humean assumptions. For Hume causal relations consisted of 1) a noted temporal precedence and 2) regular succession. In other words, a causal relation is established when an initial event occurs before a second event (temporal precedence) and, whenever the first event occurs, it is followed by the second one (regular succession). With this Humean conception of causality, there may be good grounds for expecting an event to occur but not for explaining *why* it occurred. In contrast, the realist would look for causal connections between the two "events." The realist would ask why and how this temporal precedence and regular succession occur and would in the process inquire into the presence and kind of particular causal mechanisms. There are other differences between the realist and positivist accounts, but this distinction is, I believe, sufficient to deflect the charge of "positivism" and helpful enough as an indication of where I am headed.

The meaning of functional explanation

At times functional explanations appear to be odd statements. Common sense would seen to indicate that if something is explained by its effect, the assertion is that the effect "caused" the event. When functional explanations are interpreted in this manner, the criticism is that such explanations entail an illicit backward causation. Something that comes later cannot "cause" an event that occurred earlier. Functional explanations also appear to be specious statements that on closer inspection fail. Consider the following "explanation" of schools. Capitalist society requires a legitimation of its social order. Schooling encourages people to believe that we live in a just society. "Therefore" schools exist to legitimate capitalism. Schools are "explained." But have schools been explained? For certain critics functional explanations are specious and entail claims of backward causation. Still, properly constructed functional explanations are comprehensible and plausible explanatory forms. They do not imply illicit causal claims nor are they necessarily specious statements.

Some examples of functional explanations include:

- Giraffes have long necks because the effect of an elongated neck enables them to survive in their environment (Darwinian Functional Explanation).
- A capitalist set of production relations develops in conjunction with a set of productive forces because this

> set of production relations has the effect of furthering
> the productive forces (Cohen-Marx Thesis of Functional
> Compatibility).

- When a set of production relations fetters (contradicts)
  the growth of the productive forces, a new set of
  production relations evolves that is conducive to the
  development of the productive forces (Cohen-Marx
  Thesis of Functional Contradiction).

- The structure of public schooling alters because the
  effect of such change sustains economic growth (Bowles
  and Gintis' Thesis of Historical Correspondence).

- Accounts of conflict in the natural and social science
  curricula of the elementary public schools are absent
  because their absence has the effect of stabilizing
  capitalist social relations (Apple's Thesis of a Selective
  Tradition).

All of these statements are presented as hypothetical conjectures,
not warranted explanations. And all of these conjectures conform
to the pattern of proper functional explanations: an institutional
or societal feature (or physical trait) persists because of its
consequences in a stated context.[6] Giraffes have elongated necks
because such lengths enable them to survive in an environment of
tall acacia trees. A set of production relations persists because this
set has the consequence of furthering the growth of the productive
forces. Functional explanations focus on the consequences of
events in specified contexts and state that an event persists
because of the consequences it produces. Two features are
crucial for understanding of these functional assertions. Functional
explanations identify dispositional facts and presume contextual
selection. Functional explanations entail the notion that an event
has a disposition to produce a certain effect and the assumption that
the stated context selects that event because it produces a particular
effect. Cohen's giraffe example illustrates these two assumptions:

> A population of giraffes with a mean neck length of six feet
> lives in an environment of acacia trees, on whose leaves they
> feed. The height of the trees makes it true that if they now
> had longer necks, their survival prospects would be better.
> They subsequently come to have longer necks . . . if Darwin's

theory of evolution is true, then the fact that were they to have had longer necks, they would have fared better [the dispositional fact], contributes to explaining the elongation. The environment selects in favor of variants with longer necks [contextual selection] precisely because it is an environment in which longer necks improve life chances.[7]

The conjecture that giraffes have long necks because the effect of an elongated neck enables them to survive presumes both a dispositional fact and contextual selection. Here the dispositional fact is that giraffes' survival prospects would improve if neck lengths increased: If the leaves in the trees are too high, longer necks should do the trick. An account of contextual selection is provided by Darwin's theory of natural selection. Those giraffes with longer necks live to propagate their kind and those with shorter necks die. The environment selects giraffes with the "long neck gene."

All of the functional theses stated above include a dispositional fact and a presumption of contextual selection. In the thesis of functional compatibility the persistence of capitalist production relations is explained by its consequence of furthering the growth of the productive forces. The dispositional fact is that the growth of the productive forces would be enhanced if capitalist relations were to persist. A presumption of contextual selection is also present; that is, it is assumed that the capitalist set of relations is selected, among other possible sets (e.g., feudalistic or socialistic), because of its tendency to develop the productive forces. In Apple's Selective Tradition Thesis curricula that exclude accounts of conflict are said to legitimate capitalist social relations. The dispositional fact is that capitalist social relations would secure additional legitimation if a particular curriculum were to exist. Furthermore, it is assumed that somehow curricula that will confer legitimacy are selected. Functional explanations state that because a social feature would produce an effect, that feature is selected.

Functional explanations and conflict

Critics repeatedly charge that functional explanations presume a harmoniously ordered world. Individual acts of resistance, group conflict, and structural contradictions are ignored. Sometimes this criticism is directed toward functionalism generally and not at functional explanations specifically. Functionalism, as a set of background assumptions, reputedly disregards conflict. Piotr Sztompka argues against this criticism, claiming that any paradigm of functionalism, weak or strong, views society as a set of complex elements that constitute a specific whole. Concerning this assumption of wholeness, Sztompka states:

> Two popular assumptions may thus be distinguished. The assumption of consensus claims that the relationship between the elements of the system are congenial and harmonious, and the activity of each element may be reconciled with the activities of all others. The assumption of conflict claims that such relationships are basically antagonistic and inharmonious, and the activity of the elements are mutually incompatible and divergent.[8]

Sztompka recognizes that an assumption of conflict does not typify applications of functionalism, but he argues that "the bias of functionalism in favor of consensual relations has nothing to do with the inherent properties of the systemic-functional frame of reference. The same frame of reference allows equally well a bias in favour of the conflict assumption. And it also allows for a middle position."[9] Although in the past functionalism has ignored conflict, as a set of background assumptions about society it is open to consensual or conflictual social relations.

In the educational literature the criticism frequently appears to be that functional explanations ignore conflict at the micro level. Functional explanations overlook individual students' acts of resistance. This criticism can be addressed in two basic ways, depending on the intent of the claim. When the criticism originates from an assertion that any adequate explanation of schools must take into account individuals' actions, the charge of "conflict–ignorance" is actually a minor part of a much broader position. The criticism springs from a methodological insistence on micro-reductions. According to this methodological stance, any adequate explanation of social phenomena must be reduced to the level of individual actions. If a functional explanation of schooling and economic structures does not reduce to the level of individual actions, if it does not explain the phenomenon by pointing to individual actors, it is inadequate. When seen in this light, the criticism is a minor aspect of a more central stance—an insistence on micro–reductions. I have no desire nor need to enter this classical debate. For purposes here, it suffices to illustrate that the criticism is centrally one of micro–reductions, not inattention to conflict.[10]

At other times it seems that the criticism is that functional explanations are simply not "full enough": They do not capture the complexities of public schooling. However, functional explanations are not designed to account for all aspects of reality. A single explanation or explanatory form cannot answer every question or every type of question. Functional explanations concern social and institutional features or human practices that persist over time. These phenomena are explained by highlighting their effects. Not all social phenomena can be explained in this manner, and when such explanations are put forth, only certain events are relevant to the explanation. The practice of tracking students according to ability may have the effect of supplying capital with an able and compliant work force. A functional explanation of tracking would highlight this effect and claim that it is because of this effect that the practice of tracking persists. The fact that certain students resist their placement in a particular ability group would not be pertinent to explaining the persistence of this practice.

In addition to these criticisms there is also the charge that functional explanations cannot account for structural contradictions or class conflict, notions central to a Marxist social science. In the theory of historical materialism the central contradiction refers to a structural impasse between the forces and relations of production. This impasse is the object of Cohen's thesis of contradiction. According to Cohen, Marx's theory of historical materialism includes the following functional thesis.[11] In certain societies (e.g., feudal and capitalist) the productive forces develop to a point where their further growth is fettered (contradicted) by the existing set of production relations. As a result of this contradiction, a new set of production relations evolves that is conducive to the further development of the productive forces. Formally, this functional thesis recognizes the contradiction in the economic base. Substantively, it predicts the existence of a formidable contradiction, one that implies revolutionary change. However, historically, capitalism has been able to emerge from periods of contradiction without a revolutionary alteration of the production relations.[12] The functional revolutionary thesis cannot explain the resiliency of capitalist production relations. It is at this point that a limitation of functional explanation becomes apparent.

To explain how a set of production relations is established, a Marxist approach is committed to an account of class struggle. Unless one supports a historical determinist position in which a contradiction automatically results in a revolutionary set of production relations, the outcome must be viewed as contingent on the "vicissitudes of class conflict." The result can be either a revolutionary set of production relations or a variation of the existing set of relations. A revolutionary set of production relations may enhance the growth of the productive forces only after an initial period of unproductive disorder, while a variation of the existing set of relations initially may stabilize the situation but then restrict the growth of the productive forces. In this situation of contradiction we have "competing" dispositional facts: one set of production relations will produce one general effect, and another set of relations will have a different effect. To account for the selection of one set of production relations over another, it is necessary to examine the class struggle. In a situation like this, one must account for the relative power and intentions of individual and class actors. In certain empirical situations of conflict or contradiction functional explanation may have to rely on (or possibly be replaced by) an account of class conflict. A further elaboration of this limitation requires more discussion of the structure of and procedures for assessing functional explanations. I will return to this discussion in the final section after I have examined the structure of functional explanations in the next three sections.

Cohen's defense of functional explanation

To defend functional explanations and ensure against the possibility of an illicit backward causation, Cohen argues that the structures of functional and precedence explanations are analogous. A precedence explanation is an explanation of the ordinary causal form: e occurred because f occurred since whenever F occurs E occurs. Increased learning occurred in this classroom because the students spent more time on task since, *ceteris paribus*, whenever students spend more time on task learning is enhanced.[13] And a precedence statement is explanatory when it refers to a pertinent generalization (law-statement). The precedence statement "increased learning occurred in this classroom because the students spend more time on task" is explanatory because it relates to the generalization that "whenever students spend more time on task, learning is enhanced." Similarly, Cohen argues, a functional statement is explanatory when it relates to a pertinent consequence law. "To convey the role of consequence laws in the explanation of events, we propose an analogy between 'e occurred because f occurred, since whenever F occurs E occurs'and 'e occurred because of its propensity to cause F, since whenever E would cause F, E occurs'."[14]

Consider the following example offered by Cohen. Rain dances occur in Hopi society because such dances increase social cohesion. This functional statement is explanatory because it refers to the following consequence generalization: "Whenever performance of rain dance R would bring about, shortly thereafter, a rise in social cohesion, rain dance R is performed."[15] A functional statement about the rain dance is explanatory since it refers to a pertinent consequence generalization.

On the basis of this analogical depiction Cohen maintains that functional explanations do not state that an effect "caused" an event. They do not entail an illicit backward causation.

> It is false that, in an explanation relying on such a generalization, the resulting social cohesion is put forth as explaining the performance of the rain dance. Instead, the performance is explained by this dispositional fact about society: that if it were to engage in a rain dance, its social cohesion would be increased.[16]

Further, Cohen continues:

> It can be explanatory to cite the effect of the rain dance, not because its effect explains it, but because the fact that

it had that effect allows us to infer that the condition of the society was such that a rain dance would have increased its social cohesion, and it is implied that the inferable condition occasioned the performance of the dance.[17]

The citation of an effect does not entail a claim of backward causation. Rather, the citation of an effect is explanatory because a functional explanation incorporates two elements within its structure: a dispositional fact and a presumption of contextual selection. In the Hopi example the dispositional fact is that if a rain dance were performed it would increase the Hopi's social cohesion. The assumption of contextual selection is implied but not directly identified by Cohen. Somehow the Hopi society selects the rain dance because their society is one in which a rain dance would increase social cohesion. Cohen obliquely refers to this selective ability when he states that "the condition of the society was such that a rain dance would have increased its social cohesion, and *it is implied that that inferable condition occasioned the performance of the dance.*"[18] Functional statements do not assert that an effect causes an event but rather that because an event has a disposition to produce an effect, that event is selected.

Instead of highlighting the assumption of contextual selection as a central factor in the structure of functional explanations, Cohen points to it as an element in their set of background assumptions. "The background against which consequence explanation is offered in biology or anthropology or economics is a conception of species or societies or economic units as self–maintaining or self–advancing."[19] As a background assumption for functional explanations, a conception of societal self–maintenance can only mean that within a society those events that maintain that society tend to be selected. Rain dances are selected in Hopi society because they have the effect of social cohesion. Long necks are selected for in giraffes because they have the effect of enabling survival.

Thus through analogy to precedence explanations Cohen argues that functional explanations are structurally sound and therefore do not entail an illicit backward causation. I agree with Cohen but I wish to make explicit two elements of a functional explanation, not just one. Cohen identifies the dispositional fact as the central element in the structure of these explanations. I maintain that both the dispositional fact and the presumption of contextual selection are central to a sound structural explication of functional explanations. The result of my disagreement with Cohen will become apparent in the next section.

Testing functional explanations

While functional explanations are structurally sound, whether these explanations can be empirically assessed remains a question. Functional explanations of public schools must not only be structurally sound but also amenable to testing. These explanations put forth knowledge claims about the world and as such are either more or less accurate or inaccurate. In fact, functional explanations can be assessed in light of empirical evidence, though Cohen's procedure for testing functional statements is a necessary but not sufficient means of empirical assessment.

Cohen's test of functional explanations is similar to an examination of precedence explanations. To test a precedence statement one insures that the precedence generalization on which it relies is true. Precedence generalizations have the following form: whenever E occurs, F occurs. A confirmation is accomplished by showing that whenever the antecedent (E) occurs, the consequent (F) follows, and a disconfirmation is achieved by finding instances where the antecedent (E) occurs but the consequent (F) does not follow.[20] Analogously a test of functional statements must prove that the consequence generalizations on which they rely are true. A consequence generalization has the following form: whenever E would cause F (the major antecedent), E occurs (the consequent). And, according to Cohen, a consequence generalization is "confirmed by instances satisfying its major antecedent and the consequent and disconfirmed by instances satisfying its major antecedent only."[21]

To illustrate such a test, Cohen examines a consequence generalization concerned with an expansion of scale in the shoe and garment industries.

Thus suppose we wish to test the claim that the average scale of production in the shoe industry expanded because of the economies attending large scale in that industry. We may know of the garment industry that if it were to expand the scale of its production, economies would result. So the major antecedent of this consequence law–statement, which would support the claim about the shoe industry, is satisfied in the case of the garment industry:

> Whenever an expansion of scale would lead to economies, an expansion of scale occurs.

We then predict satisfaction of the major consequent in the case of the garment industry, the fate of the prediction being a test of the hypothesized law.[22]

To confirm a consequence generalization, the correlation contained within the major antecedent and the correlation between the major antecedent and the consequent must be substantiated.

A similar procedure could be followed to examine Bowles and Gintis' Thesis of Historical Correspondence, which states that the structure of public schooling changes because the effects of such alteration sustain economic growth. The relevant consequence generalization would be that whenever a change in the structure of schooling would further the capitalist society, an alteration in the structure of schooling occurs. Following Cohen's procedure we would have to satisfy both the major antecedent and the consequent in order to confirm the consequence law. Through historical and comparative investigations the generalization would tend to be confirmed by finding that an alteration in the structure of schooling leads to (is correlated with) a further growth in the economy and that when this is the case, a change in the structure of schooling occurs. Such an assessment directly examines the correlation contained within the major antecedent and the correlation between the major antecedent and the consequent. It does not assess the selective capability of the context. The contextual selection is entailed by the consequent in the following manner. In a capitalist society, if a particular structure of schooling would further the economy, it is assumed that somehow that society selects and reinforces that structure of schooling and not some other structure.

Cohen does not disregard an examination of contextual selection. His response rests on a distinction between *why* questions and their corresponding explanations and *how* questions and their relevant answers. Functional and precedence explanations answer why questions. When answering the question Why do schools change their structure? all that is required is an appropriate and true generalization. Schools change their structure because the following generalization is said to be true: whenever an alteration in the structure of schooling would further a capitalist economy, a change occurs. That is all that is needed to answer a *why* question. For Cohen it is a distinctly different question to ask *how* that corresponding change in structure came to pass. To ask how would be to ask for an elaboration of how it is that a capitalist society is able to select that particular structure and not some other. For Cohen,

> . . . a consequence explanation may be well confirmed in the absence of a theory as to how the dispositional property figures in the explanation of what it explains. In other terms, we may have good reason for thinking that a functional explanation is true even when we are at a loss to conjecture by what means or mechanism the functional fact achieves an explanatory role.[23]

Cohen's test of functional explanations relies on an empirical assessment of the corresponding consequence generalization and ignores the selective mechanisms. When however, addressing skeptical questions about this procedure, Cohen relies not on the test as formulated above but brings in an examination of the context's selective capability. The problem with Cohen's proposed test is that it is possible to confirm a false consequence generalization. One can identify a strong positive correlation between the major antecedent and the consequent in the consequence generalization but find that a hidden variable is actually the cause of both the major antecedent and the consequent. A functional explanation of ability grouping in public schools might state something like the following: Ability grouping in public schools occurs because such practices supply capital with a skilled and compliant work force. The pertinent consequence generalization would state that whenever ability grouping would be beneficial for capital, it occurs. Graphically this can be depicted as

(If E were to occur, it would lead to F)———→E occurs.
Where E represents the practice of ability grouping and F the noted positive effects for the economy.

However, it is conceivable that there is some other variable —G— responsible for both the major antecedent and the consequent, for both the practice of ability grouping and the positive effects. It is not unreasonable to envision a society with a traditional belief in hierarchical divisions among its members. It is possible that this traditional belief is responsible for the practice of ability grouping, and in turn the ability grouping positively effects the economy. Furthermore, it could be that actions based on this traditional belief, and not the dispositional fact (the correlation contained within the major antecedent), cause the subsequent practice of ability grouping. Graphically this is represented as

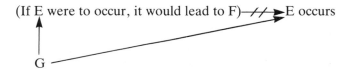

(If E were to occur, it would lead to F)—//—►E occurs

G

Where E represents the practice of ability grouping, F the stated positive effects for the economy, and G the tradition of hierarchical divisions.

This example illustrates that it is conceivable to have a true consequence generalization but a spurious functional relation if another intentional variable is present and responsible for both the major antecedent and the resulting consequent.

Cohen accepts this possibility but argues that such situations cannot be generalized to all functional explanations. "It is false that dispositional facts are never more than concomitants of what functional explanations claim they explain."[24] To prove his point, Cohen provides the giraffe example that I quoted earlier. I include the entire example now since it shows that when arguing against the possibility of a non-functional, causally relevant variable, Cohen emphasizes the environment's selective capability. He relies on Darwin's theory of natural selection to substantiate the truth of this functional explanation. To wit, Cohen's example undermines his argument against identifying an elaborating theory.

A population of giraffes with a mean neck length of six feet lives in an environment of acacia trees, on whose leaves they feed. The height of the trees makes it true that if they now had longer necks, their survival prospects would be better. They subsequently come to have longer necks. So far all we have is evidence of a consequence generalization. But if Darwin's theory of evolution is true, then the fact that were they to have had longer necks, they would have fared better, contributes to explaining the elongation. The environment selects in favor of variants with longer necks precisely because it is an environment in which longer necks improve life chances. On no construal can the dispositional fact be reduced to an unexplanatory precursor of the acquisition of the feature. Its explanatory relevance to the elongation of the neck is entailed by the Darwinian Theory.[25]

Here Cohen states that an elaboration of the contextual selection is necessary to substantiate the functional explanation of the giraffes' necks. An identification of the selective mechanism shows that it is because of the environment's ability to select the dispositional tendency, and not some other variable, that longer necks appear.

The giraffe example constitutes strong prima facie evidence against Cohen's formal position that an identification of mechanisms is not required to test functional explanations. When pushed, Cohen examines the assumption of selection. Cohen's stated procedures for testing are further undermined when we examine the difference between the background assumptions of precedence and functional explanations.

As I noted earlier, Cohen relies on an analogy between precedence and functional explanations to argue for 1) the formal adequacy of functional explanations and 2) the procedures to test functional explanations, and furthermore, Cohen states that all explanations operate against a set of background assumptions. The cogency of Cohen's analogy between functional and precedence explanations begins to falter when we examine their respective sets of background assumptions. Functional explanations assume a context of self–maintenance. No analogous assumption is entailed by precedence explanations. Due to the lack of an analogical counterpart in precedence explanations, the assumed similarity of procedures to test these explanations is called into question.

Recall that Cohen proposes an analogy between precedence and functional explanation: "To convey the role of consequence laws in the explanation of events, we propose an analogy between 'e occurred because f occurred, since whenever F occurs, E occurs' and 'e occurred because of its propensity to cause F, since whenever E would cause F, E occurs.'" A test of any explanation involves an examination of its corresponding generalizations (law statements). With precedence explanations one must show that if F were to occur, E also occurs. With functional explanations it is necessary to confirm that if E would cause F, E occurs. In both cases one must confirm the respective law–like statements. Structurally, the requirements are similar. However, entailed in the meaning of a consequence generalization is the proposition that because E would cause F, E occurs. The only way I can make sense of this phrase is to assume a context of self–maintenance such that E is selected because E confers a beneficial effect within the stated context. Precedence generalizations do not contain an analogous assumption. Since this assumption is present in consequence generalizations but not in precedence generalizations, one would assume that appropriate tests of the respective generalizations must differ accordingly. Cohen assumes that no important distinctions occur and therefore constructs structurally analogous tests. However, as I have shown, Cohen's procedure for testing consequence generalizations relies on an assumption of contextual selection, and when pushed, Cohen examines the context's selective capability.

Both the giraffe example and the highlighted incongruity belie Cohen's assertion that an adequate test of functional explanations need not identify suitable mechanisms. Jon Elster, Anthony Giddens, and Philippe Van Parijs have criticized Cohen for his inattention to selective mechanisms.[26] Unfortunately, these critics either assume the need for elaborations or bring to the debate substantially different assumptions. Van Parijs begins to address the problem directly when in a footnote he indicates:

> Cohen argues that "functional explanations may reasonably be proposed, in light of suitable evidence, but in advance of an elaborating theory." . . . But it is precisely because such "suitable evidence" is bound to be lacking, at least in nonexperimental disciplines, that I believe Elster's position on this issue is right (the need of an elaborating theory).[27]

I will argue that an adequate test of functional explanations in nonexperimental disciplines requires an elaborating theory. In order to know whether or not Marxist functional claims about schools are more or less true or false, it is useful to identify the operating selective mechanisms.

Functional explanations and selective mechanisms

In order to rule out the possibility of a non–functional (e.g., intentional) explanation and adequately test a functional explanation it is necessary empirically to assess 1) the correlations asserted in a consequence generalization and 2) the selection implied in these consequence generalizations.

Functional statements assert that since a particular event produces a certain effect, that event is selected. Cohen's test examines the correlations contained within the consequence generalization. One must satisfactorily prove that 1) E leads to F and 2) when E leads to F, E occurs. A difficulty arises when it is pointed out that even when the correlations 1) and 2) are confirmed, an intentional rendition can account for the event's appearance. The possibility that another variable is responsible for both the major antecedent and the consequent stands as a non-functional alternative hypothesis. Ruling out alternative accounts is one of the basic procedures for testing explanations. If functional explanations are to be confirmed, one must confidently preclude the possibility of a non–functional, intentional account. Cohen's prescribed methodology is generally unable to rule out these alternative accounts.

In the experimental sciences alternative hypotheses are ruled out through the device of the experiment, an artificially constructed setting through which an investigator achieves the required degree of control successively to eliminate rival accounts. This procedure is available to certain disciplines within the natural sciences. However, in the social sciences, rigorous experimental designs that could achieve the required degree of precision are not feasible and are frequently ethically questionable. In the social sciences rival accounts cannot be eliminated through rigorous experimentation. The social sciences must rely on reasoned argumentation, employing statistical techniques and historical and comparative investigations. If the elements within a correlation can be specified in a sufficiently precise manner, statistical techniques and historical and comparative investigations may be able to rule out alternative accounts. When this is possible a degree of confidence can be achieved. However, it is difficult to imagine a potentially true consequence generalization about social phenomena whose correlations could be specified with the necessary precision. It is always a distinct possibility that some other variable is responsible for both the major antecedent and the consequent. Another procedure is required to achieve the desired specificity and thereby eliminate alternative non–functional accounts.

Through citing the selective mechanism, one achieves the desired specificity and therefore the ability to eliminate non–functional (intentional) alternatives. The difference between a functional and an intentional explanation is this: In the functional explanation an institutional feature is said to persist because it produces a particular effect, because of its dispositional tendency, whereas a direct intentional explanation of the same event would claim that the actions of social actors are directly responsible for the dispositional fact and the resulting event. By hypothetically identifying and confirming a functional mechanism of selection, one is able to illustrate the distinctly functional character of the relationship and show that it is by virtue of a functional selective mechanism, and not some other variable, that the event persists. An investigation of mechanisms must be accompanied by fairly reliable correlations. Without a sound dispositional fact (the correlation contained within the major antecedent), there would be nothing to select.

Mechanisms of social selection

Thus far I have argued that functional explanations are structurally sound and empirically examinable. While in order to test functional explanations it is crucial to advance plausible mechanisms, if the need to cite mechanisms is accepted, a further problem arises: Can suitable social mechanisms be formulated? Although social mechanisms can be identified, in fact, the potential use of functional explanation in Marxist analysis of schools is limited. Functional explanation in the social sciences is warranted by two general types of mechanisms: a social version of natural selection and reinforcement mechanisms. The major obstacle in utilizing functional explanation in the social sciences is that frequently a direct intentional mechanism can account for the beneficial effect, thus supplanting a functional explanation. When intentional mechanisms can be cited that account for the noted beneficial effect, there is no need for recourse to the complexities of functional explanation: An intentional explanation will suffice. Therefore, although functional explanation is a structurally sound explanatory form and, when applicable, a powerful explanatory tool, its use in the social sciences is limited.

Functional explanations of biological evolution are warranted by a theory of natural selection. Social theorists have borrowed this theory of selection and applied it to societal examples with limited success. To date, Van Parijs has provided the most promising formulation of a set of selective mechanisms. He asserts, and I agree, that his elaboration of reinforcement mechanisms represents "the most significant mechanisms for . . . legitimating social scientific functional explanations."[28] The best way to facilitate an understanding of these mechanisms, and in turn to illustrate the limited applicability of natural selection and reinforcement mechanisms, is initially to outline the theory of natural selection.

Generally the theory states that biological organisms develop particular physical and behavioral traits because of the traits' adaptive value. A trait first appears as a result of chance variations in the organism's genetic code and persists because environmental factors endow it with survival value. Returning to Cohen's giraffe example, random genetic variation would create the initial appearance of various neck lengths, and the environmental presence of tall acacia trees would favor those giraffes with longer necks. Longer necks enable these giraffes to eat, thus survive and reproduce. In short, long–necked giraffes are selected. Two characteristic features of this selection process need to be highlighted: First, natural selection consists of the specification of some trait (longer necks, to use Cohen's example) through selecting the appropriate organism (giraffes with longer necks); and second, natural selection accomplishes this specification of a trait through endowing the appropriate organism with enhanced survival possibilities.

A similar scenario illustrates the selection of profitable firms within a competitive economy. Suppose there are a number of competing companies producing miniature toy giraffes. We can presume that some of these companies would enhance their profit if they increased their scale of production, thereby reducing their production costs and enhancing their profits. Because of the lower retail price of these firms' miniature stuffed giraffes, their giraffes are purchased rather than those produced by the firms that did not increase their scale. Eventually, the former firms dominate the market, and the latter companies declare bankruptcy. In this social example of "natural selection," the two characteristics are present. First, certain companies are selected because of their profitable practices. The selection is for a particular feature (increased scale), through the "choice" of an institution (certain types of firms). Second, the criterion of selection between firms is one of survival. Those companies that increase their scale prosper and those which do not fail.

While the theory of natural selection warrants functional explanations in evolutionary studies, it has only a very limited application to functional explanations in the social sciences. Social selection does not frequently operate through a criterion of differential survival nor does it seem to select an institution because it contains a particular feature. Marxist explanations of public schooling do not indicate that without the practice of ability grouping schools would cease to exist, but rather that the practice of tracking in schools is conducive to the stability of a capitalist society. Nor do Marxist explanations suggest that tracking is selected through the selection of the institutions of schooling, but rather Marxist claims suggest that the institutional feature of tracking is selected directly.

To accommodate social selection, Van Parijs develops a conception of selection as a set of reinforcement mechanisms. He states:

> Reinforcement, to start with, is a generalization of operant conditioning that can be roughly characterized as follows. Whereas natural selection and its analogues always consist in the selection of some item (e.g. market behaviour) through the selection of an entity (e.g. a firm) it characterizes, reinforcement consists in selection of an item (e.g. habit) directly within the entity concerned (e.g. an organism).

Three related differences immediately follow from this basic contrast. Instead of natural selection's chances of reproduction, reinforcement involves the operation of some "choice" criterion internal to the entity, say its "chances of satisfaction." Further, reinforcement requires the registration, however dim and sporadic, of the causal link between the item and its functions, whereas no awareness whatsoever is required by natural selection. Finally, reinforcement warrants the explanation of changes taking place within a particular entity, and not just in a population of entities (or a representative member of it).[29]

Reinforcement mechanisms operate through a criterion of satisfaction, entail an initial but subsequently diminished awareness of the link between the practice and its beneficial consequences, and select the practice directly. The criterion of satisfaction is a standard of minimal, not optimal, satisfaction. A social practice could fulfill this criterion if it selected out the decidedly dysfunctional elements, thus reducing the potential for crisis: In the theory of reinforcement crisis reduction is equivalent to minimal satisfaction. In natural selection the selection criterion is survival: A feature persists if it enables the organism to survive and thus reproduce. In cases of reinforcement a feature persists if it satisfactorily reduces the potential for crisis. The second major difference between reinforcement and natural selection is that whereas natural selection need not entail any awareness and conscious choice, social reinforcement entails an initial but subsequently diminished awareness of the link between the practice and its beneficial consequences. The subsequent lack of awareness is essential for the credibility of a functional–reinforcement elaboration. If the persistence of the beneficial effect can be attributed to the actors' conscious choices, then an intentional, not functional, explanation should be offered. If conscious choice is involved, it is not necessary to have recourse to the complexities of functional explanation. A more direct and simple intentional explanation will suffice. If, however, the intentions of actors cannot account for the persistence of an institutional feature or practice, it is quite possible that the feature persists due to it beneficial consequences. The third and final criterion is that in reinforcement elaborations the practice or feature is selected directly and not through the selection of institutions that contain that feature. In social instances of natural selection firms that practice increased scale are selected, whereas in reinforcement elaborations the practice is selected directly. Since all of this is rather abstract, I think a few illustrations would be helpful.

Three hypothetical explanations for the practice of ability grouping (tracking)[30] in public schools follow. In the first case a clear and strong example of social reinforcement is postulated, in the second case a mixed (reinforcement and intentional) elaboration is offered, and in the third case an intentional elaboration supplants the functional-reinforcement mechanism. These examples will illustrate 1) how reinforcement mechanisms operate and 2) how intentional explanations coincide with or supplant functional-reinforcement explanations.

Case 1. It seems reasonable to postulate that ability grouping in the elementary and secondary public schools has had the beneficial effect of producing a minimally skilled and differentiated work force. In this first case a functional explanation of tracking would claim that the tracking has persisted due to its beneficial effects for preparing capitalism's future workforce. A functional-reinforcement mechanism would have to present a scenario similar to the following story: Tracking was initially instituted as a result of business organizations' efforts and involvements in the schools. In lieu of an adequate intentional account and with sufficient historical documentation, the persistence of ability grouping could be explained not as a result of any continued efforts or actions by powerful organizations, but rather because it has provided a minimally skilled and differentiated work force, thereby reducing the propensity for economic crisis. To make the argument for the continued presence of a functional-reinforcement elaboration stronger, it needs to be the case that even after actions are taken to replace ability grouping with another method of instructional organization, the practice of tracking persists. If these conditions hold, then it would seem that tracking persisted and continues to persist because of the beneficial consequence it provides for the economy.

Case 2. Again it seems reasonable to postulate that ability grouping in elementary and secondary public schools has the beneficial effect of providing a minimally skilled and differentiated workforce. Furthermore it seems plausible to suppose that tracking, relative to other available options, provides an efficient means for distributing educational resources. In this second case the persistence of tracking could be explained 1) in terms of its beneficial effects for capitalism and 2) as a result of the conscious efforts of school personnel to maintain a feasible approach to the distribution of educational resources. The citation of a functional beneficial effect follows the elaboration outlined in Case 1: tracking persists in part because it provides a minimally skilled and differentiated workforce and thus contributes to a crisis-free economy. However, a second non-functional, intentional mechanism can also be cited. School administrators and teachers perceive tracking as the best means, among possible options, for distributing educational resources to groups of differentially talented students. In this intentional explanation tracking is said to persist because school personnel desire a satisfactory means of instructional organization. They perceive tracking as the most satisfactory approach, and tracking is said to persist, in part, due to their inter-ests in maintaining it. In this second case the explanation offered depends upon a combination of mechanisms: both intentional and functional-reinforcement mechanisms are cited.

Case 3. Finally a third hypothetical explanation is possible. As in the previous two examples, tracking can be described as having the beneficial effect of providing a minimally skilled and differentiated workforce. However, rather than postulating that tracking persists due to these beneficial effects, it could be possible that tracking persists as a result of business' concerns for their future workers and parents' concerns for their children's futures. Instead of a functional-reinforcement a direct intentional explanation could be offered. Both business organizations and parents push to satisfy their respective goals. Business desires at least minimally skilled workers and parents desire children qualified and skilled to work. Both business groups and parents are aware of the link between eduction and work in a capitalist economy. "Better" curricula mean enhanced business and a knowledgeable child secures a profitable job. Tracking is perceived as a fair and efficient means to achieve these respective goals. Thus, tracking is explained as an outcome of actions that have as their goals the same effect cited in the functional explanation. When actors intend the beneficial effect cited in a functional explanation, there is no good reason to offer a functional explanation. In these cases an intentional explanation supplants a functional one.

These three cases illustrate how a functional-reinforcement mechanism might operate and how it is possible for an intentional explanation to coincide with or supplant a functional explanation. Two additional points can be drawn from these examples. First, one can begin to see how attempts at examining functional explanation, ascertaining the presence or absence of a functional mechanism, can lead to political action. In effect, an attempt empirically to assess a functional explanation can lead to the heralded Marxist "pragmatic" test of a theory. Second, these three cases underline the limitations of functional explanation in the social sphere.

In the first case I noted that in order to strengthen the argument for a functional-reinforcement elaboration, political action oriented toward instituting a dysfunctional (crisis producing) educational approach would have to fail. In effect the "test" of a functional-reinforcement elaboration might "call" for political and social action. An illustration should be helpful. Let us suppose that the working and affiliated classes want to replace tracking with an alternative educational approach. Rather than continuing to track students, these class actors propose a method of instructional organization that is individualized in its assessment of needs and abilities and cooperative in its instructional approach as well as encouraging a norm of cooperation between individuals. Further, let us suppose that in addition to replacing ability grouping, they propose a curriculum that aims to educate morally autonomous thinkers who value a communitarian ethos. Now if such an agenda were supported with sufficient strength, conflict would most probably ensue. One would expect the proposal to be opposed by business leaders and possibly state officials. If conflict erupted, a functional approach could not account for or predict the outcome. Much depends on the nature of the conflict and the distribution of resources and power.[31] Once the conflict was resolved, it would still remain to be seen whether an intentional or functional explanation is appropriate. If business interests were able to sustain tracking as a form of instructional management and delivery and if their active support for tracking subsequently ceased and tracking persisted, then it would seem that a functional-reinforcement mechanism would be a prime candidate. If the working and affiliated classes prevailed, a class-intentional reading would seem more appropriate. Empirically examining functional explanations is not a simple matter, though such examinations can "lead to" pragmatic tests and show at times how functional explanations cannot account for the outcome of conflict.

Conclusion

In this chapter I presented functional explanation as a defensible but limited form of explanation. I maintained that these explanations are structurally sound and empirically assessable and outlined a preliminary approach for examining the evidential basis for functional claims. In Chapter 2 I argued that Marxist explanations of public schools, while critical of functional approaches, nevertheless rely on functional assertions and ignore rigorous empirical assessments of these claims. It now seems appropriate to recognize the limitations of functional explanations. Marxist analyses of schools can utilize functional explanations but their use must acknowledge the restrictions placed on these forms of explanation. In the next chapter I will examine Michael Apple's functional assertion linking curricula to capital, arguing that the connection between curricula and capital is best viewed as a combination of functional and intentional mechanisms, and I will provide a conceptual framework and a methodological procedure to assess these claims.

4
Is there a selective tradition?

Marxist analyses of schooling assert that the public school curriculum is a product of a "selective tradition." In these accounts the knowledge included in and excluded from the curriculum represents a selected body of information and skills that is "connected" to the reproduction of class domination. Those who outline this connection between curricula and capitalism generally assert the presence of a functional relationship. A curriculum persists because it is conducive to capitalist society. While several studies have critically examined the schools' curricula, these analyses have not adequately connected the presence or absence of curricular topics to capitalism.[1] The connection to the logic of capital is asserted but not substantiated. As I have argued in Chapters 2 and 3, without an indication of how this functional relationship is maintained, we are left with an interesting thesis but without an adequate appraisal of whether or not this functional nexus actually exists. These assertions must now become the object of disciplined examination. In this chapter I will not attempt to prove that the curricula-capitalism connection exists. I will, however, provide a conceptual and methodological framework whereby these assertions can either be adequately substantiated, qualified, or discarded.

There are two interrelated claims contained within the analyses of the selective tradition. First, there is the assertion that a functional relationship exists between the schools and capitalism: The curriculum is beneficial for the maintenance and progress of capitalism and persists because it is beneficial. The second claim is that elements in a curriculum that would obstruct a capitalist mode of production are identified as being dysfunctional to capitalism and therefore are excluded from the public school curriculum. The assertion that the curriculum represents a systematic elimination of curricular topics entails a very specific judgment: What is excluded from the curriculum is just as important as, if not more important than, what is included. Any attempt to substantiate these functional assertions confronts particular difficulties. Conceptual problems are posed by the task of identifying how this selection occurs and how it is connected to the logic of capital, and methodological dilemmas are encountered by efforts to explain what is excluded.[2] Neither the conceptual nor the methodological problems have been confronted within the radical curriculum literature.

There are areas to which we can look for help in this matter. Peter Bachrach and Morton Baratz[3] have analyzed comparable dilemmas in their studies of community power, and Claus Offe[4] has highlighted similar conceptual and methodological issues in his study of state power. In particular, Offe's analysis identifies a number of conceptual reconstructions and methodological tools that can be used to explain the selection of curricular elements. It will therefore prove helpful to examine Offe's analysis in order to reconstruct the conceptual basis and then construct the methodological strategies conducive to an explanatory account of the selective tradition.

The analysis will proceed as follows. First a critique of the existing literature will be offered: My criticism is that functional assertions[5] are substituted for adequate explanations. Two theses are then offered as a basis for transforming these assertions into a plausible explanatory account. The first thesis states that when claims of a functional relationship are made, it is helpful to identify the probable mechanisms (both functional and intentional) that could maintain a causal connection.[6] The mechanisms must point to the linkages between schools and capitalism. The second thesis states that the most useful way to conceptualize and identify these mechanisms is through viewing schools as state institutions. Within this framework the potential exists for a more adequate identification of the exclusionary mechanisms and therefore of the connection between capital and the schools.

Finally, with the critique outlined and the theses stated, Offe's analysis will be employed to construct the framework for an adequate explanation. His analysis provides the skeletal approach for investigating the claims of selectivity and for remedying the peculiar difficulties of an analysis of negative selection.

By employing Offe's conceptual apparatus and following his methodological prescriptions, a framework will be established whereby the functional claims of the selective tradition can be put to realistic examination.

The selective tradition

The analysis of a selective tradition came to the foreground of curriculum scholarship with the publication of Michael Apple's *Ideology and Curriculum*. In the introductory chapter Apple describes the curriculum as a composite social product whose selection and organization are formed from all of the "available social knowledge at a particular time and place."[7] Employing Raymond Williams' notion of a selective tradition, whereby a dominant class creates and recreates the conditions for its privileged position, Apple argues that the crucial task for curriculum scholarship ought to be the identification of how the selective tradition operates in the public school curriculum. For this to be accomplished, Apple states, we need to identify the connections 1) between the organization and selection of curricular knowledge and schools and 2) between schools and other economic and political structures.[8] The identification of the linkages between schools and curricular knowledge and the larger economic and political structures would illustrate how educational institutions "act as powerful agents in the economic and cultural reproduction of class relations."[9]

In curriculum studies the analysis of the selective tradition can be characterized by three distinct but interrelated claims. First, there is a basic working assumption that the curriculum is a body of knowledge that represents a selection from "all possible knowledge." Second, it is asserted that a functional relationship exists between the curriculum and class relations. This second claim entails at least three subsidiary claims: selection is class biased; as such it is beneficial for a capitalist society; and these selections occur because they are reproductive. The third premise is that the curriculum creates the ideological conditions necessary to reproduce capitalist social relations. The asserted quality of the functional claim and the ideological characterization are highlighted when Apple states:

> The selective tradition . . . is a "natural" outgrowth of
> the relations between our extant cultural and economic
> institutions. . . . When a society "requires," at an economic
> level, the "production" of agents who have internalized
> norms which stress engaging in often personally meaningless
> work, . . . then we would expect that the formal and informal
> curricula, the cultural capital, in schools will become aspects
> of hegemony. . . . Any other response will seem unnatural,
> which is exactly the point both Williams and Gramsci have
> maintained.[10]

Recently Apple has extended his analysis of the general school-capital nexus to include accounts of contradiction, resistance, and struggle.[11] However, the mechanisms through which schools and their curricula are connected to class relations remain unexplored. Without such investigations any claims for the existence of a selective tradition are seriously undermined.

This inattention to mechanism is present in recent curricular analyses. Jean Anyon has produced two studies that point to the selective nature of the public school curricula. In "Ideology and the United States History Textbooks" she demonstrates that accounts of economic change, labor history, and social conflict are absent in high school social studies texts, and in "Elementary Schooling and Distinctions of Social Class" she points to the selective nature of the elementary school experience and curriculum as it is differentiated along lines of class.[12] Joel Taxel has noted the selective nature of children's literature according to race and gender and on the topic of the American Revolution.[13] Frances Fitzgerald, with less theoretical development than the other writers, has identified the historical predominance of inclusionary and exclusionary practices in the production of social studies textbooks.[14] While all of these analyses "point" to examples of the selective nature of curricular materials, they share an identifiable weakness. All of the work (with the obvious exception of Fitzgerald's atheoretical presentation) relies on the assertion of a functional relationship between curriculum and capitalism to explain the absence or presence of curricular topics. The missing accounts of economic change or social conflict in schools' curricula are "explained," automatically, as a result of the functional connections between schools and capital. What is functional for capital is included in the curriculum, and what is dysfunctional for capital is excluded from the curriculum. However, before any warranted claims can be made about the curriculum, a causal connection between capitalism and curriculum must be established.

In order to examine this purported connection between schools and capital, it is necessary to reconstruct the conceptual foundations of the selective tradition literature. Two theses are important. First, rather than automatically assuming a functional relationship, operating mechanisms must be identified that link schools to capital. And second, in order to identify the mechanisms, it is advantageous to view schools as state institutions. A brief elaboration of these two theses should sufficiently ground an approach to the curriculum so that Offe's analysis can be employed to create an explanatory framework.

Two theses

The *first thesis* criticizes the assertion of an automatic functional relation between curricula and capital and calls for the identification of a set of plausible causal mechanisms connecting capital and curricula. Rather than defining the selective tradition in a manner that presupposes a functional, much less an automatic functional connection, it seems more plausible initially to search for both functional and intentional mechanisms. The essential defining characteristics of a selective curricular tradition would no longer assume a functional tie but would stipulate that 1) the curriculum is a body of knowledge selected from all possible knowledge; 2) a causal connection exists between curriculum and class relations; and 3) the curriculum creates effects beneficial to capitalist social relations.[15] With this definition both intentional and functional mechanisms can now be postulated.

In order to ascertain whether a selective tradition operates in the public school curricula, it is necessary first hypothetically to identify plausible causal mechanisms and then to determine their empirical presence. As I argued in Chapter 3, in order to establish the claims of a distinctly functional relationship, the noted beneficial effect cannot be an intended outcome of any group or class, and a functional mechanism must be cited. While it is logically possible that the relation is distinctly and singularly functional, given the limitations of social functional explanations one would expect intentional explanations to supplement, at least, the causal account. Two additional types of explanations are possible: a mixed explanation or a distinctly intentional explanation.

In a mixed explanation the functional claim would be that aspects of the selective curriculum persist because of the beneficial consequences for capitalism. The intentional claim would be that the selections are the direct outcomes of actions that are unintentionally beneficial for capital. Teachers may support tracking because of its positive effects for classroom order and not because tracking has beneficial consequences for capitalism. A distinctly and exclusively intentional explanation would claim that the curricular selections are chosen because of their beneficial effects. I propose that the selective tradition in public school curricula is an outcome of mixed and intentional mechanisms. An empirical examination of this claim would first identify probable mechanisms and then proceed to assess the explanation by empirically confirming or disconforming the acclaimed mechanisms. This means that the asserted causal connection between capital and school curricula will find corroboration or falsification to the degree that appropriate functional-reinforcement, social "natural" selection, or intentional mechanisms linking curricula to capital can be reasonably postulated and empirically examined. If mechanisms cannot be ascertained, the claim of a selective tradition is seriously weakened. The first thesis calls for a search for specific mechanisms ensuring the persistence of a selective tradition.

The *second thesis* identifies schools as state institutions. Within the schooling literature, Roger Dale, Martin Carnoy, and Henry Levin point to the appropriateness of examining schools as part of the state apparatus.[16] There are many institutional levels within the state, and certainly schools must be located accurately therein. Nevertheless, it is difficult to dispute the conceptualization of schools as tax-supported institutions. Viewing the schools as state institutions, the potential exists for a more adequate identification of the exclusionary mechanisms. Dale states that this placement allows for a framework that "can explain patterns, policies and processes of education in capitalist societies more adequately than existing approaches."[17] Such an assertion requires careful inspection, and yet I agree with Dale (and with Carnoy and Levin) that an analysis of the state-schooling nexus should provide more satisfactory conceptual tools than either a casual disregard of this apparent context or a conception that places schools within a distinctly different setting.

With these two theses stated, the construction of a conceptual and methodological framework can be initiated. What is needed now is a route by which the ascription of a causal relationship can be examined. Offe's analysis provides the tools appropriate for an investigation of the exclusionary mechanisms.

Offe's analysis: the selectiveness of the state

Offe's framework can be utilized most effectively by initially presenting the skeletal logic of his argument and then employing the key elements of his paper for an analysis of the absences in curricula. In "Structural Problems of the Capitalist State—Class Rule and Political Systems: On the Selectiveness of Political Institutions," Offe undertakes an analysis of the State in capitalist societies. His article provides the conceptual tools for the identification of links between capital and the state in advanced capitalist countries. The framework is elaborate, and for my purposes it will be substantially distilled.

Offe's basic claim is that there are structural power linkages between the state and capital (as a class) such that state institutions selectively exclude anticapitalist interests. Such a claim can be easily misconstrued, so it is important to note that Offe's argument does not assert a tightly knit functionalist thesis between the state and the economy, nor does it claim that all of the state's actions are to be seen as functionally explained by the capitalist economy,[18] and it also does not assume a smooth operation in fulfilling any functional requirements. Instead, Offe's analysis assumes that, given the power of the capitalist class and the role of the state in helping minimally to maintain capitalism, state institutions tend toward excluding events dysfunctional to capitalism. Class conflict and contradictions arise over attempted selections, and the state is not always successful.

Support for Offe's thesis can be outlined by following four basic steps. Initially it must be shown that linkages of structural power between the state and capital do exist. Without this condition it would be absurd to contemplate the occurrence of state selection in any way that could be described as causally related (functionally or intentionally) to the capitalist economy. The second step involves two basic formulations: the state is designated as a system of sorting and selecting rules, and the capitalist state is further specified as involved in a particular type of selection—systematic selection. Only when the selection is tied to the interests of capital as a whole can it be said to be systematic. Under this requirement it must be shown that the state selects out those policies and practices that would damage the long-term accumulation of capital and those divisive strategies or interests that would be dysfunctional to the legitimation of capital.

The third step in Offe's argument is the identification of a set of "nested filters," the mechanisms through which negative selection occurs. At the most general level, selection occurs as a result of the structural connections between the state and capital. Because of the state's dependence on capital accumulation for its own revenue, certain selections will be made. If the dysfunctional elements are not excluded by the structural mechanisms, they may be filtered at the level of ideology. That is, due to the assumptions people have about their social world, their relationships to this social world, and the everyday practices that engender these assumptions, a selective perception is generated. A third level of selection occurs at a procedural level. The institutional rules and processes establish an agenda whereby certain interests are given priority and others are excluded. The final level is the repressive mechanism: certain events are excluded as a result of direct force or repression.

With these mechanisms identified, Offe advances to the fourth and final proposition in his analysis. While the claim of operating mechanisms can be theoretically asserted, it must confront the empirical world. Admittedly, the "confrontation of theory and 'fact'" is never a simple task, and within the framework of negative selection particular methodological problems are encountered. Here the crucial dilemma centres on the sociological identification of excluded events: How does one establish the "presence" of non-events? Offe's position is expressed best in the following statement.

The historically concrete limits of a system of political power can only be perceived as a political practice and can only be identified in the class conflict engaged in through action and organization in which collective normative options turn into an empirical force. The class character of the State becomes evident analytically only in an ex post perspective, namely when limitations of its functions become apparent in class conflict.[19]

Offe's claim is that the exclusionary character of the state, and for us the curriculum, can only become evident through an identification of class conflict over potential selections. This empirical investigation must be supported by the conceptual framework of filter mechanisms. The selective limitations imposed by the state are revealed in at least two ways: When conflicts erupt between classes, either previously institutionalized state selective mechanisms exclude the dysfunctional element or a new mechanism is established by the state. This framework does not assume success on the part of the state, nor does it presuppose that the state attempts to exclude all dysfunctional elements.

The investigation of the selective tradition's claims will follow a route similar to Offe's analysis. To move from the realm of theoretical assertions to an empirical investigation requires 1) identifying the structural linkages between schools' curricula and a capitalist economy; 2) indicating that in the process of curriculum production those elements that would be dysfunctional for capital legitimation and accumulation are systematically excluded; 3) identifying the possible mechanisms at work; and 4) confronting the conceptual and methodological issues posed by an investigation of nonevents. Within these four areas, an empirical investigation of curriculum production will be suggested.

Structural linkages

Since any investigation of the class-bound character of curriculum production depends on the presence of linkages between schools and the capitalist economy, it will be useful to identify at least three "sites" where such connections occur. The connections between the production of curricular guidelines and materials within the schools and related state institutions (e.g., in the United States, departments of public instruction) *and* the capitalist economy can be located in at least three different types of relationships. The linkages can be seen at the points where business strategies focus on individual teachers; where civic and business organizations push for their own class interests in local an state school governance bodies (e.g., in the United States, school boards and state legislatures); and where corporate publishers of texts and curriculum materials interact with the local and state identification of curricular guidelines.

It has been noted that smaller business and larger corporate entities concern themselves with the individual teacher. In his article "Curricular Form and the Logic of Technical Control," Apple begins his discussion by outlining a corporate strategy known as the "Ryerson Plan."[20] The stated goal of this plan is the eradication of a purported anti-business and anti-free-enterprise bias in American society. Through the "education" of school teachers in summer workshops, corporate representatives attempt to influence the curriculum. Although it is not Apple's purpose to highlight this connection, it is clear that here a linkage exists between schools and the class-based corporate structure. Another example of this type of connection can be found in the non-educationally based corporate production of low-cost, and at times free, curricular materials. Multiple examples of this type of curriculum production can be found in Sheila Harty's *Hucksters in the Classroom: A review of Industry Propaganda in the Schools.*[21] Both of these examples highlight one type of linkage between a capitalist economy and the schools: business organizations focus on the individual teacher.

A second type of connection can be seen in the class-backed organizational attempts to exclude particular texts and formulate broad curricular aims. These political strategies are usually focused on the local school boards and the state legislatures. The class character is readily apparent for some of these struggles, but for other initiatives more careful examination is necessary. The history of the successful exclusion of Harold Rugg's extremely popular social studies text from the public schools during the 1930s and 1940s is one example in which the class connection is apparent. Viewed by the Advertising Federation of America and the National Association of Manufacturers as a highly subversive textbook, the repeated publication of their charges of sedition reduced the use of the text to a point where it was no longer published. School boards did not want to purchase seditious texts. While in the late 1930s the series was quite popular, by the late 1940s its sales declined drastically as, Fitzgerald notes, the "textbook market took a sharp rightward turn."[22]

Another link between the curriculum and the capitalist economy can be seen where the corporate production of textbooks and curricular materials connects with the state and local guidelines for curriculum selection. Fitzgerald has noted that the guidelines for textbook adoption have a marked effect on the corporate production of texts.[23] Publishers produce books that meet the perceived guidelines and attempt to copy previously adopted texts. Once a text is adopted by a "super" state (e.g. Texas, Florida, or California), it is frequently adopted by other states.[24] Apple has noted that in this process there are positive economic gains for both the publisher and the local school districts.[25] Publishers benefit from the adoption of their textbooks, and where a state subsidization of approved texts exists, the monetary benefits are shared by the local school district. While much of this situation has not been analyzed by radical curricular theorists, this connection between corporate publishers and state and local guidelines represents a third linkage between schools and a capitalist economy.

Systematic selection

A primary effect of these various linkages between schooling institutions and the capitalist economy is, as Offe puts it, the "privileged consideration of particular interests and influences."[26] And in order to see how this privileged consideration operates, it is helpful to view educational institutions as state institutions involved in a selection process. The selective tradition's claim would be that this selection allows the capitalist class to gain a privileged position. An investigation of this claim would have to identify whether, and if so, how, this selection allows a priority to capitalist interests.

In this selection process, there is a universe of possible events that will be excluded. Some exclusions could be connected to capitalist interests, while others could be the outcomes of forces unrelated in any direct or indirect manner to capital. Due to the range of possible exclusions, it is helpful to differentiate between three different types of selection: sociohistorical, accidental, and systematic. The first two types of exclusion are not connected to specific class interests; systematic selection is.

Curricular topics that are excluded because of the sociohistorical premises of a society and/or the systematization and development of knowledge in a society are topics that are negatively selected but not tied to a capitalist economy. In the United States, an advanced capitalist country, the public schools do not teach incantations for faith healing, the alchemic properties of pewter, or the tribal lineages of its students. This type of exclusion is not an outcome of any particular tie that schools have to capital. Rather, these curricular topics appear to be excluded due to the premises of what is justifiable knowledge or the result of a particular sociohistorical juncture. The continuing debates over values and sex education and over evolutionary theory in biological studies appear to fall within this realm. It is difficult to construe these debates and conflicts as emanating from a logic of capitalism.

Accidental exclusions are those events that are negatively selected because of the contingent features of curriculum pro-duction. These events could have come into existence without violating sociohistorical premises or conflicting with the structure or the procedural rules of the institutions. The recent presence of sand and water tables in United States primary schools was once thought to be the result of the influence of the British infant school movement. Yet these curricular devices could be found in rural Wisconsin schools at the turn of the century. These pedagogical tools were part of the elementary curriculum in the past, were later excluded, and now again can be found in the primary levels of some schools in the United States. Their inclusion has not altered the institutional structure or the procedural rules of the school. It appears that there is a range of curricular topics whose inclu-sion or exclusion is based on pedagogical considerations. These pedagogically motivated selections can be seen as outcomes of the contingent aspects or the sociohistorical premises of curriculum production.

Whereas neither sociohistorical nor accidental selections can be connected to the logic of a capitalist economy, systematically excluded events are generated directly by the schools' structures and processes as political systems and arise out of the linkages of power between schooling institutions and structures of class interests. And yet systematic selection is not defined solely as those selections that arise out of the structural linkages between schools and capital. If the schools and their curricula are to be identified as institutions in a systematically selective state, the schools must not only be linked to capital but also be shown to select out those events that are dysfunctional to the creation of the conditions for the reproduction and production of a capitalist system. Two types of dysfunctional selection are important: It must be shown that curriculum topics that would damage the long-term accumulation process of capital are excluded and that the curriculum topics that are divisive or oppositional to the legitimation of capitalist production are also excluded.[27]

The mechanisms

Systematic selection can be analyzed as operating through a system of four kinds of filter mechanisms. Offe's claim is that these mechanisms are organized as a nested set of filters in a sorting process. As noted earlier, the mechanisms operate at four different levels: structural, ideological, procedural, and repressive. Through this hierarchical layer of filters the curricular topics that are dysfunctional to capital could be excluded. To understand how these mechanisms operate two steps must be taken. In this section I will describe each mechanism, characterize it as mixed or intentional, and point to possible class connections. In the next section I will note how these mechanisms are to be connected methodologically to class.

At the structural level it can be seen that schools are articulated to labor markets and capital accumulation in two significant ways. Labor markets place specific limitations on the schools: curricula should engender minimally skilled and knowledgeable workers. Schools are also structurally dependent on capital accumulation through the means of public taxation. These two features impose limits on the curriculum. Dependent on capital accumulation for their revenues, schools are sensitive to the needs of capital. Business organizations form coalitions with schooling institutions to identify the necessary skills for the labor force. Due to the nexus of schools and the labor market, parents are concerned that the schools' curricula focus on the fundamental working skills of its classed populations. It appears that in the face of the possibility of capital flight or parental disapproval, the curriculum is structurally predisposed to the interests of capital. This particular filter represents an intentional mechanism. Business organizations, parents, and/or school personnel take steps to select out material viewed as unfavorable to the preparation of future workers or children's futures as workers.

While the scope of possible curricular topics is limited initially by the structural articulation of schools, labor markets, and capital accumulation, the curriculum is restricted further by a system of ideological norms. At the ideological level, limitations occur through the promotion of what Offe calls a "selective perception and articulation of social problems and conflicts."[28] To borrow from Goran Therborn's analysis of ideology, the schooling population's perception of what exists, what is good, and what is possible, when applied to the selection and creation of curriculum materials, limits the possibilities for a broader scope of curriculum materials and practices.[29] In our educational system a strong emphasis on the norms of cooperation or critical analyses of capitalism are not thought to be appropriate educational concerns. Many parents and school personnel believe that our society is a free and competitive one that, while not the best of all conceivable worlds, is generally fair and bound to outlive us all. Since a competitive economy exists and seems fair and since this economy, it is believed, will persist, most people think it is reasonable that students be prepared to compete in the existing system. Curricula that do not enable such participation are excluded. Characterized in this manner the ideological filter is an intentional mechanism: people act on their beliefs to exclude material that harm students' futures in a capitalist society.

Selection also occurs as a result of institutional procedures. Offe states that "every procedural rule creates conditions of being favored or conversely being excluded for certain issues, groups or interests."[30] This mechanism can be seen in the state adoption procedures of curricular materials. Twenty-one of the fifty states require state approval of curricular materials. This centralized structure allows either highly limited local participation or choice from a list of state-approved materials. California and West Virginia have a dual selection structure between the state and local laws, and the remaining twenty-seven states allow local selection.[31] The states with a centralized structure limit the direct political participation in curriculum formation and thereby enlarge the radius of bureaucratic action. This limit has an effect on those states with local policies. Given the requirements for capital accumulation, the publisher will produce with an eye to the largest and most secure market—the centralized states. The effect is that curriculum materials available for those states with local policies will have been previously selected by publishers producing for centralized states. In those school districts where teacher participation in the creation of curricula is sanctioned by state and local regulations, teachers are allowed to present curriculum materials for approval through a complex system of committee meetings. Some teachers, overworked in many areas, decline the invitation to sit through review committees and fill out the required forms.[32] Those teacher-initiated materials that have followed the procedures tend to conform to the formats of existing curriculum materials. Teachers know that material that mimics established curricula is given priority. Other materials are thereby excluded.

The procedural filter is a combination of functional and intentional mechanisms. At the publishing level textbook selection appears to follow a reinforcement elaboration. A profitable textbook must satisfy many divergent and conflicting consumer demands. Only those texts that satisfy the lowest common denominator of all contending forces will sell. A junior high social studies text with selections from H. Rap Brown, Karl Marx, and Fidel Castro would not be purchased whereas a text with rather uncontroversial content would. Safe texts are produced because they minimally satisfy the greatest number of people. In this example the process of selection matches the criteria for a functional-reinforcement scenario as outlined in Chapter 3: Texts are produced that reduce the potential for crisis within the schools; publishers may desire to publish less "safe" texts but are compelled, because of the market, to publish uncontroversial texts; and finally the selection is for safe texts and not firms that produce the texts. Other procedural filters can be illustrated using functional-reinforcement elaborations, but intentional mechanisms also seem present. The example of teacher participation in text selection relies on an intentional reading. Given the constraints under which teachers work, it is understandable for teachers not to participate in the available avenues for text selection or curriculum design. And when they do participate, it is not surprising that they mimic already established curricula. Teachers may not desire to select out certain material but a result of their inaction or mimicry would be continued selection of dysfunctional content.

The final level of selective filtration is the limitation imposed through suggested or implemented acts of repression or force. Dismissals of politically active teachers have occurred throughout the history of schooling in the United States, and books have been removed from school libraries. In the earlier part of this century, New York City teachers were fired because of the allegedly critical content of their curricula.[33] Throughout this century school officials and parents have illegally taken materials out of the school libraries. This repressive mechanism represents an intentional mechanism: active or threatened repression excludes curricular options and is intended to exclude these options.

Methodological dilemmas

These four levels of selection illustrate the possible mechanisms of exclusion, but as noted above, they are not adequately connected to capital. To assert a claim of systematic selection, these exclusions must be shown to be nonaccidental and dysfunctional for capital accumulation and legitimation. An identification of the mechanisms is, by itself, insufficient to argue the systematic nature of selection. The mechanisms must be shown to select out those curricular topics that are dysfunctional to a capitalist economy. This problem represents one methodological obstacle in the attempt to link the methodological dilemma posed by the study of "nonevents." Any attempt to show the nonaccidental, class-related character of the exclusions must employ concepts that point to what is excluded. Offe has a solution. The identification of the class character of curricular exclusions is accomplished by investigating the normatively expressed and observable instances of class conflict. The only way adequately to substantiate the nonaccidental and dysfunctional nature of the exclusions and confront the problems posed by the status of nonevents is to identify the exclusionary mechanisms in operation in political practice. For, as Offe reminds us, it is only when class conflict occurs that the implicit class options turn into empirical force, and it is only during these times of class conflict that the ruling class character of the state becomes evident. Offe's methodological route focuses on the eruption of class conflict, that is, on times of crisis. This does not mean that all investigations of the selective nature of the curriculum must focus on times of crisis. However, through an analysis of expressed class conflict over curricular aims, content, and practices the attempted exclusions can become an objective and identifiable focus of struggle, the mechanisms can be identified, and the class character of the selections can be confirmed. The analysis of normal periods can note the continued presence or absence of the mechanisms, but—and this must be stressed—any such analysis needs to rely on studies of overt conflict to link the mechanisms to class. A limited example of how this research agenda could progress can be seen in a historical analysis that highlights the role of class conflict over curricular aims and content. Julia Wrigley's examination of the Chicago school system presents some tentative leads as it focuses on class conflict and identifies the creation of procedural selective mechanisms.[34]

A historical example

In a study on the politics of the Chicago school system from the turn of the century to the years following World War II, Wrigley found that organized labor and business organizations battled over the control of the curriculum. One of the areas of conflict concerned proposals made by Chicago's Commercial Club and other related capitalist interest groups to create a dual system of academic and vocational education. The proposal was visibly resisted by the Chicago Federation of Labor and the Illinois State Federation of Labor, which opposed the plan for the reorganization in explicit class terms: such a dual system would confine their children's futures but not the futures of the children of members of the Commercial Club. Another area of contestation between labor and business was the content of the public schools' curricula. Labor supported a "fads and frills" proposal that extended the scope of the curriculum beyond the basic, rudimentary skills. The employers' organizations wanted to limit the curricula of the public schools to the "Three R's." In both of these areas of conflict, labor pressed for an extension of offerings to working class students, while the business organizations pushed to limit the aims and content of the working-class schools. Workers did not want their children's futures tied to the needs of capital, and the capitalists did not want an ill-trained and dissatisfied work force.

What is important for our purposes is Wrigley's identification of a selective mechanism that was created to limit the educational programs. The original site of class conflict was the open political arena of the community, and the conflict focused on the decision-making status of the school board. Due to the initial defeat of the employers' proposals, the business groups altered their strategies, and, according to Wrigley,

> . . . instead of provoking direct conflict, as the Commercial Club had done, the business groups in most cases attempted to work with middle-class civic organizations to secure revision of the structure of the school system. The goal of "efficient" school administration was common to both and provided justification for many changes that met with business approval.[35]

In this account bureaucratic procedural mechanisms were instituted as a result of the conflict between labor and business organizations. Defeated in the open political arena, business organizations joined forces with the "middle-class civic organizations" to create procedural mechanisms that accomplished their procapitalist goals.

Wrigley's study emphasizes both the class conflict and the creation of a procedural mechanism. The connection between selection and class is accomplished by linking the empirically identifiable class antagonism to the institutionalization of a procedural selective mechanism. The business groups achieved their goals and excluded labor's opposition by instituting a plan of "efficient" school administration. Wrigley's account provides a historical example of curriculum selection in which class conflict results in the establishment of a procedural filter. In this example the selection is beneficial for capital since it excludes labor's dysfunctional opposition. The creation of the procedural mechanism is explained as an outcome of powerful business actors who were able successfully to reduce labor's opposition by locating future decisions within the school bureaucracy. The persistence of this procedural mechanism may be given a functional-reinforcement reading: Locating the decision-making process within a bureaucratic apparatus reduces the likelihood of crises erupting between labor and capital and thereby helps to maintain capital's power; such effects are no longer actively sought by business interests; and the procedure was selected directly and not through the selection of the institution in which it is contained. In this example it seems that all three criteria for a reinforcement mechanism are met. It seems that Wrigley's account provides an example of how curriculum selection can be viewed as a procedure of systematic selection. The selection is beneficial for capital since it excludes labor's potential opposition, and the mechanism can be identified and adequately connected to class interest.

Conclusion

In this chapter I have constructed a conceptual and methodological framework through which the claims of a curricular selective tradition can be examined. I have formulated an approach whereby the assertion of a capitalist curriculum can be confirmed, disconfirmed, or reformulated. In general, my presentation, with its use of substantive examples, has given credence to the claim that aspects of the public schools' curricula are selected products tied to a capitalist economy. However, the major reason for entering into a re-examination of the claims of a selective tradition has been to provide an explanatory framework more amenable to empirical corroboration or falsification. Sociological argument about curriculum production must begin to pay heed to the empirical rigor of any reputable scientific endeavour. Given an explanatory framework, the validity of the argument must now rest, to a great degree, on whether or not these selective mechanisms can be empirically identified and tied to a capitalist economy.[36] If this can be accomplished, serious consideration should then be given by those outside the tradition of Marxist scholarship to the claims of a selective tradition. If this cannot be accomplished, those working within the critical tradition will have seriously to revise their theoretical framework and empirical claims.

This call for explanatory rigor need not preclude the traditional Marxist concern for praxis—for informed political action. In both this and the previous chapter I've indicated how evidential examinations can lead to social and political action. In effect, the examination of an explanatory conjecture, functional or intentional, need not result in academic quiescence or resignation. Social and political conflict can provide further information about the presence and strength of an acclaimed mechanism. If it is posited that tracking or particular administrative procedures are functionally related to capitalism, one should examine the recent and historical record for evidence. One could also "test" the strength of the proposed mechanism by organizing social efforts to establish oppositional practices, practices dysfunctional to capitalism and favored for other attractive features (e.g., non-ability grouped cooperative classroom instruction or more direct democratic decision-making procedures). However, whether or not these organizational efforts ought to be undertaken cannot be answered by an appeal to evidence. At this point the Marxist researcher confronts an ethical question. Whether one organizes or partakes in oppositional practices cannot be decided by the "facts." These are peculiarly ethical dilemmas, and their justification depends on moral deliberation. In the next two chapters I examine the Marxist tradition's ethical foundations, and its ability to answer these and related ethical questions.

5

Ethical values and
Marxist educational critiques

Marxists attempt not only to explain capitalism, but also condemn capitalism as a social formation and call for the transformation of capitalism to socialism. Similarly Marxist educators criticize schooling in a capitalist society, attempt to explain its dynamics, and call for the transformation of public schooling and the larger society. In Chapters 2, 3 and 4, I examined the Marxist explanatory project. In this chapter and the next, I will analyze both the evaluative and prescriptive components of a Marxist theory of schooling.

In a very real sense the evaluative and prescriptive features of Marxist theories provide the motivation for the radical project. Explanations, by themselves, have little value unless they serve to enhance our social and political well being. Marxist functional explanations, as I have refined them, may enable a clearer understanding of the ways in which schools and capitalism unduly constrain children's future lives. If this understanding is to be translated into avenues for political and social action, however, an adequate understanding of the moral basis of the Marxist explanatory project would be helpful. This moral basis is a central feature of the Marxist project. In order to act on our explanations, we must understand and lay claim to our moral beliefs, and in order to know what to explain, we must be directed by our moral sensibilities.

When educational institutions and practices are condemned as pernicious and prescriptions are outlined to transform public schooling, two questions are appropriate: What are the criteria (what is the basis) for the condemnation? Do the proposed changes satisfy or at least not conflict with these criteria? It seems unreasonable morally to criticize capitalist schools without acknowledging the criteria behind the appraisal or issue educational proposals that are not in accordance with these criteria. In this chapter, I will identify the potential criteria, and in Chapter 6 I will examine the use of these criteria to propose changes in the public schools.

Generally Marxists condemn capitalism and schooling in capitalism as a form of injustice. Capitalism is a system of economic expropriation in which one class, due to its position within a structure of economic relations, dominates and exploits the labor of another class. In capitalism social relations also mask (mystify) these underlying relations. In a capitalist society the social relations conceal class domination and exploitation. Usually the ethical content of such concepts as domination, exploitation, and mystification and their connection to justice are not rigorously analyzed. It is assumed that these forms of social relations are unjust and that therefore capitalism is unjust and morally culpable. Marxist educators claim that the structure of the larger socioeconomic system is unjust and that schools contribute to the reproduction of this unjust system.

These claims of injustice can be found in different degrees in almost any Marxist analysis. The critiques vary from straightforward but unexamined condemnations of capitalism and schooling, to explicit but incomplete examinations of the moral basis for the condemnation. Paul Willis and Samuel Bowles and Herbert Gintis criticize the inequalities of schooling in a capitalist society and by implication condemn capitalism for its injustices. However, neither Bowles and Gintis nor Willis examines the basis for this condemnation. The apparent general and shared assumption is that schooling in capitalism subjugates individuals to an exploitative and unequal social system and that such forms of domination and inequality are morally reprehensible. They do not state baldly that inequality and exploitation are morally pernicious, but it is difficult to construe their meaning in any other fashion. For example, Bowles and Gintis state that "Repression, individual powerlessness, inequality of incomes, and inequality of opportunity do not originate historically in the educational system, nor do they derive from unequal and repressive schools today. The roots of repression and inequality lie in the structure and functioning of the capitalist economy."[1] Willis argues that members of the working class, although struggling for freedom, are nevertheless inserted into a system of exploitation. He writes:

> The astonishing thing . . . is that there is a moment . . . in working class culture when the manual giving of labor power represents both a freedom, election and transcendence and a precise insertion into a system of exploitation and oppression for working class people. The former promises the future, the latter shows the present. It is the future in the present which hammers freedom to inequality in the reality of contemporary capitalism.[2]

There is a pervasive message in these authors' works: Capitalism is characterized by unequal, repressive, and exploitative social relations, schools help to reproduce these relations, and such a social system is unfair and unjust.

Whereas Bowles and Gintis and Willis highlight moral standards through a critique of capitalist social relations, Henry Giroux emphasizes the moral element through a comparison of theoretical frameworks. Giroux contrasts the "positivist" and "critical" approaches to school and society. For Giroux positivism separates questions of "fact" from questions of value, emphasizes the factual realm and as a result suppresses ethical concerns. Since this theoretical framework separates what Giroux believes are integrally related concerns, another approach is necessary. Contrasted to the positivist framework is the critical approach of the Frankfurt School. Critical theory does not separate "fact" from "value." Instead, critical theory is

> . . . tied to a specific interest in the development of a society without injustice. . . . [That is,] critical theory contains a transcendent element in which critical thought becomes the precondition for human freedom. Rather than proclaim a positivist notion of neutrality critical theory openly takes sides in the interests of struggling for a better world.[3]

While it is not clear what the "transcendent element" is in critical thought that functions as the precondition for human freedom, it is clear that Giroux's critical theory must be morally informed and rooted in notions of social justice and freedom.

Another prominent analyst, Michael Apple, argues that a standard of justice is integral to the study of schooling in a capitalist society. For Apple the explanatory and evaluative components of Marxist analysis are intertwined.

> To hold our day-to-day activities as educators up to political
> and economic scrutiny, to see the school as part of a system
> of mechanisms for cultural and economic reproduction, is
> not merely to challenge the prevailing practices of education.
> . . . the kinds of critical scrutiny I have argued for challenges
> [sic] a whole assemblage of values and actions "outside" of
> the institution of schooling. . . . It requires the progressive
> articulation of and commitment to a social order that has as
> its very foundations not the accumulation of goods, profits,
> and credentials, but the maximization of economic, social,
> and educational equality.
>
> All of this centers around a theory of social justice. My
> own inclination is to argue for something left of a Rawlsian
> stance. For a society to be just it must, as a matter of both
> principle and action, contribute most to the advantage of
> the least advantaged. That is, its structural relations must be
> such as to equalize not merely access to but actual control of
> cultural, social, and especially economic institutions.[4]

The commonly accepted basis for Marxist condemnations appears to be a mixture of a rather broad standard of social justice and an elementary conception of freedom. While these claims appear to accord with a general interpretation of the Marxist tradition, they are not developed in any substantial manner and, in fact, are far from secure. Recently, writers have argued that Karl Marx did not and that a coherent Marxist social theory cannot condemn capitalism for alleged injustices.[5] There are at least three distinct positions in this argument.[6] First, in what is generally known as the Tucker-Wood thesis, Allen Wood maintains that Marx's condemnation was not an assessment related to a criterion of justice and furthermore was *not* even a *moral* condemnation. (In this chapter I will discuss specifically Wood's argument since it represents the most recent and sophisticated version.) According to this view, Marx believed that all moral criticism was a form of moralism, an ideological and ineffective type of social criticism. Marx's own critique, the argument goes, was based on rational, not moral criteria. A second position, the Anti-Justice thesis, is neutral with respect to whether Marx's condemnation was moral but maintains that Marx was an outspoken and thorough critic of calls for social justice. According to this position, Marx refuted attempts to critique capitalism for its allegedly unjust and inequitable distribution of social goods or any purported violation of equal rights. Such criticisms, Marx thought, missed their mark and were inherently flawed. The third position, the Human Nature thesis, argues that Marx's critique was morally grounded, not on a standard of justice, but rather on a conception of human freedom. From this point of view, a naturalist ethic constitutes Marx's underlying ethical basis. While men and women are beings who have the capacity for freedom, the ability to control and direct their lives, capitalism frustrates this capacity, and for that reason, Marx morally censured capitalism. Within the literature on Marx and morality these three theses are prominent and should be addressed. In the following three sections I will argue 1) that Wood's anti-moral reading is untenable, 2) that Marx was indeed skeptical of critiques based on a notion of justice, and finally 3) that Marx's condemnation of capitalism was a moral assessment based not on a standard of justice but rather on a conception of human freedom.

What lies ahead is a general analysis of the Marxist tradition's ethical foundations, not oriented specifically toward schools. Given the current state of the educational literature, such discussions are necessary. The normative foundations of radical educational thought have not been developed. If theorists criticize schools utilizing aspects of the Marxist framework, it makes good sense to understand that framework's ethical criteria. My discussion will indicate that although there is no solid consensus on the ethical basis of the Marxist tradition, the standard of justice (a standard frequently used by Marxist educational theorists) does not fare well. I do *not* argue, via the "authority" of Marx, that since the Marxist tradition criticizes the notion of justice it cannot or should not be used. Instead, I maintain that 1) the Marxist tradition presents an unusual and powerful critique of the justice standard, one that merits inspection; 2) researchers utilizing this tradition ought to be aware of this critique; and finally 3) if this critique conflicts with researchers' own notions, then they should present arguments in defense of their own ethical criteria.

Wood's thesis

Allen Wood argues that Marx did not morally censure capitalism, did not employ a moral standard of social justice, and, furthermore, when Marx spoke of justice, he utilized a sociological (juridical) conception of justice.[7] Accordingly, for Marx social relations are "just" when they correspond and "unjust" when they conflict with the existing mode of production. Wood maintains that Marx did not employ a moral standard of justice to condemn capitalism. Instead, when Marx "condemned" capitalism, his critique was based on rational, not moral, criteria. Marx judged all moral criticism of capitalism to be ideological and therefore incapable of affecting worthwhile social change.

I think it is only fair to note that for many readers Wood's interpretation initially appears counter-intuitive. To say that a condemnation does not entail a moral judgment and that justice is not a moral standard violates ordinary usage. Usually condemnations and deliberations about justice imply moral discourse. We tend to think of moral discourse as entailing the use of standards to judge whether an obligation is owed, as a consideration of the value of particular virtues and vices, or as an examination of the consequences of certain social arrangements. In each of these cases judgments are made whether a particular action, virtue, or arrangement is good or bad, right or wrong. With respect to Marx, Wood does not share this conception. It is therefore important to understand that Wood interprets Marx as stipulating a particular, and unusual, definition for each of the following terms: to condemn is to assess, employing rational not moral standards, and a just society is one in which the social relations correspond to the productive forces.

To support a juridical as opposed to an ethical reading of Marx's concept of justice Wood quotes, and I will follow, a passage from the third volume of *Capital*.

The justice of transactions which go on between agents of production rests on the fact that these transactions arise as natural consequences from the relations of production. The juristic forms in which these economic transactions appear as voluntary actions of the participants, as expressions of their common will and as contracts that may be enforced by the state against a single party, cannot, being mere forms, determine this content. They merely express it. This content is just whenever it corresponds to the mode of production, is adequate to it. It is unjust whenever it contradicts that mode. Slavery, on the basis of the captalistic mode of production, is unjust; so is fraud in the quantity of commodities.[8]

Wood interprets Marx as saying:

The justice of the transactions in capitalist production rests on the fact that they arise out of capitalist relations, that they are adequate to, and correspond to, the capitalist mode of production as a whole. The justice of property rights based on labor in a system of individual private property arises from the fact that these rights correspond to the production relations of individual producers each owning the means of production he uses. By the same token, then, the reversal of these property rights under capitalism is equally just. Capitalism is made possible by the existence of labor power as a commodity, by its use as a commodity to produce surplus value and expand capital. Labor power could not even appear as a commodity if there were no surplus value created by it for capital. Therefore, if there were no surplus value, if the workers performed no unpaid labor and were not exploited, the capitalist mode of production would not be possible. Under a capitalist mode of production the appropriation of surplus value is not only just, but any attempt to deprive capital of it would be a positive injustice.[9]

In addition Wood argues that for Marx

. . . justice is not a standard by which human reason in the abstract measures human actions, institutions, or other social facts. It is rather a standard by which each mode of production measures itself. It is a standard present in human thought only in the context of a specific mode of production.

Hence there are no general rules or precepts of "natural justice" applicable to any and all forms of society.[10]

For Marx, according to Wood, a society is just if its social relations correspond to the mode of production.

Wood further argues that Marx did not employ the concept of justice in the usual manner because Marx believed moral criticism to be ideological. For Wood the claim that moral beliefs are ideological translates into the assessment that morality is idealist, functional for capitalism, and false. This means that morally to condemn capitalism for exploiting and dominating the working class is a form of "historical idealism." Moral critics of capitalism "regard the moralistic approach to social criticism as predicated on the belief that the faithful adherence to the current moral precept is the proper way to effect progressive social change and to remove social oppression."[11] Ethical criticism is idealist since it implies not an alteration of the relations of production but a transformation of consciousness. Secondly, moral norms "can be explained by the way in which they sanction existing social relations."[12] A society's moral beliefs are codified within its legal norms, and according to Wood's reading of historical materialism, the legal structure sanctions existing social relations. Morality is functional for capitalism.[13] Finally, moral beliefs are false, illusory, since "people are normally unaware of the social function fulfilled by the moral convictions they hold, and ignorant of the real basis of the high minded sentiments which motivate them."[14] In sum, moral talk is ideological twaddle.

Whereas moral criticism is ideological, Wood maintains that Marx's own critique was rational and therefore not ideological. Wood argues that Marx condemned capitalism for violating nonmoral goods. "Marx bases his critique of capitalism on the claim that it frustrates many important (nonmoral) goods: self-actualization, security, physical health, comfort, community, freedom."[15] Although other ethical analysts and Marxist exegetes view self actualization and freedom as morally good, Wood does not.[16] Wood limits moral goods to beliefs and actions that are valued because "conscience or the 'moral law' tells us we ought to."[17] A "nonmoral good" is something we value "because it satisfies our needs, wants, or our conception of what is good for us."[18] Self actualization, security, and freedom are goods that men and women "need" but are not prescribed by moral law, and as such they constitute "nonmoral goods." A society that does not promote or frustrates the fulfillment of these needs is, according to Marx (as interpreted by Wood), irrational.

Finally, Wood maintains that Marx consistently criticized those who employed the moral criteria of justice or rights to condemn capitalism. "Marx in fact regarded all attempts to base revolutionary practice on juridical notions as an 'ideological shuffle,' and he dismissed the use of terms like 'equal right' and 'just distribution' in the working class as 'outdated verbal trivia.' "[19]

Wood's argument initially appears plausible and persuasive. Yet Marx did frequently denounce capitalism and capitalists on moral grounds. Wood acknowledges that Marx's "writings seethe with moral indignation, apparently directed against the bourgeoisie and its apologists,"[20] but argues that his interpretation can account for Marx's moralistic reaction. Wood states that

> . . . we can account for the tone of Marx's writing quite well if we suppose that his indignation is directed primarily against those "oxen" who "turn their backs on the torments of humanity and care only for their own hides." Callousness in the face of suffering is a nonmoral evil. Marx falls into no inconsistency if he morally condemns an attitude of complacency in the face of massive and remediable nonmoral evil, while refusing to condemn morally the nonmoral evil itself.[21]

While Marx may not morally condemn suffering and deprivation, Wood does admit that Marx "morally condemns an attitude of complacency." If moral talk is ideological twaddle, then Marx's moral anger must be viewed as inconsistent with his exclusive emphasis on rational criteria. But Wood concedes no inconsistency.

> When Marx says that all morality is class morality and that justice consists in correspondence to the prevailing mode of production, he means that the effect of moral standards as a whole is to protect prevailing social relations and that certain distinctive features of prevalent moral ideas (e.g. the justification of self reliant individuality in bourgeois morals, or the emphasis on the sanctity of private property)

can be explained by the way they promote class interests. But it does not follow from any of this that each and every element of bourgeois morality counts as distinctly bourgeois considered in isolation from the whole or that the moral precepts preached in bourgeois society always promote bourgeois interests whenever followed. Bourgeois morality, for instance, also teaches virtues such as kindness, generosity, loyalty and fidelity to promises. But there is no reason to think that these teachings, in their bare bloodless generality, are peculiar to bourgeois society or necessarily serve bourgeois interests.[22]

Wood's qualified definition of morality and its connection to capitalism is untenable for it is obviously inconsistent with his earlier blanket statement that "morality may be described as ideology."[23] One cannot reasonably hold both positions.

The inconsistency of these two positions can be highlighted by pointing to the implications of Wood's qualified definition of morality for his earlier argument characterizing morality as ideological. In fact, if we accept Wood's new formulation, his previous argument fails. First Wood argues that since moral discourse is functional for capitalism, moral criticism is invalid. Now Wood maintains that not all moral precepts are functional for capitalism, and therefore only those moral sentiments that serve bourgeois interests are ideological and invalid. This altered conception of the relationship between morality and capitalism allows for the existence of moral beliefs that not only do not serve but are dysfunctional for capitalism. In principle, this formulation allows for the possibility of dysfunctional moral standards of justice, and in fact, there are principles of justice that are decidedly dysfunctional for capitalism. Wood's earlier characterization of moral standards of justice as ideological can no longer be sustained.

Wood might concede the possibility of a non-functional moral principle of justice, but presumably he would argue that for Marx moral critiques of capitalism remain ideological since they imply an idealist, and not a materialist, route for social change. Purportedly, moral criticism always implies that social change occurs either through an adherence to the "correct" moral beliefs or as a result of an alteration of individuals' ideas or sentiments. Such a view is certainly questionable. It is indeed possible to condemn capitalism as unjust without implying that an alteration of capitalism requires only a change of moral attitudes or beliefs. Wood is rather equivocal here. While acknowledging that moral critics of capitalism are not "necessarily committed to this belief when they base their criticism on 'justice' or other moral ideals," he maintains nevertheless that "it is undeniable that the belief is commonly held by people who do adopt a moralistic approach to social issues."[24] Wood's argument is not sound. Since moral criticism does not necessarily (conceptually) entail an idealist commitment, moral critiques cannot be faulted for an inherent commitment to idealist routes for social change. Furthermore, it is simply false to reason that since moralists have been committed to an idealist view of social change in the past, they will do so in the future. There is no good reason to assume that if two beliefs were conjoined in the past, they will also occur in the future. Moral criticism may have been idealist but it need not always be idealist.[25]

At least one notion of justice as formulated by Kai Nielson, neither implies an idealist route for social change nor is functional for capitalism. One of Nielson's two principles[26] states:

> Each person is to have an equal right to the most extensive total system of equal basic liberties and opportunities (including equal opportunities for meaningful work, for self determination and political and economic participation) compatible with a like treatment of all. (This principle gives expression to a commitment to attain and/or sustain equal moral autonomy and equal self-respect).[27]

This principle neither legitimates a capitalistic mode of production nor implies an idealist route for social change. A social system granting each person an equal right to political and economic liberties would probably be a society that practiced political and economic democracy.[28] A program of economic democracy conflicts with the current capitalist economic oligarchy: It would be dysfunctional for capitalism. Furthermore, the attainment of economic democracy, while certainly requiring a change of values, cannot rely solely on an alteration of moral precepts. Derek Shearer and Martin Carnoy have outlined major structural and institutional changes that would have to accompany a struggle for economic democracy in the United States.[29] Obviously, Nielsen's first principle of justice cannot be characterized as either functional or idealist.

Thus, moral principles need not be ideological. Specifically, not all principles of justice are necessarily functional for capitalism, nor do they entail an idealist approach for social change. Wood's argument that Marx's condemnation was not a moral critique is inconsistent and not convincing. I have not examined Wood's position that Marx construed justice as a relation of correspondence and need not do so here.[30] Presently, there are more pressing concerns. In particular, there are a number of writers who portray Marx as a skeptic of justice-based social criticism. While these analysts differ on whether Marx's condemnation was "moral," they agree that Marx wrote disparagingly of criticisms based on appeals to schemas of equal distribution or equal rights. If justice is construed as entailing demands for an equal distribution of goods or equal rights, it can be argued adequately that Marx decried both notions as standards for assessing societies or institutions. If this is so, then contemporary Marxists will have either to revise the basis for their condemnation or to construct a substantial justification for the use of justice and its related notions to criticize schooling in a capitalist society.

The anti-justice thesis

Frequently Marxists are viewed as putting forth the following claim: Capitalist society is characterized by an inequality of basic social goods and resources, and it is this inequality in the distribution of goods that must be rectified; if the distribution were made more egalitarian, then all would be fine and fair. In response to such claims Marx was quick to point out that the central inequalities in the distribution of goods in a capitalist society arise not from the vagaries of distributive schemas but from the structure of the mode of production. In capitalism the inequality of social goods and resources is the result of the inherent conflict between capitalists and workers. Whenever the mode of production is characterized by class antagonisms, the distribution of goods and resources will be unequal. According to Allen Buchanan, this view constitutes one of Marx's most central and radical criticisms of capitalist society:

"One of the most serious indictments of capitalism—and of all class-divided societies—is not that they are unjust, but that they are based on defective modes of production which make reliance upon conceptions of justice necessary."[31] And furthermore, "The demands of justice (here distributive equality) cannot be satisfied in the circumstances which make conceptions of justice necessary, thus efforts to achieve justice inevitably fail."[32] As long as the productive structure of any society is characterized by class conflict, Marx believed that demands for distributive justice would be issued but not satisfied without a basic revolutionary change in the mode of production.

One might reasonably conclude that if calls for distributive equality require an alteration in the production relations, then the injustice of capitalism lies not in the distributive system but within the relations of production. Here the critique would state that the wage contract between capitalist and worker is unjust. The worker is paid a specific wage in return for his or her labor power, but the worker creates a value greater than that for which he or she is paid. Surplus value is extracted from the worker. The injustice lies in the "fact" that the exchange between the capitalist and worker is not equal. This situation violates the right of the worker to an equal exchange. While this claim is frequently heard in Marxist circles, it seems evident that for Marx the exchange is fair and just[33] and does not violate any rights of the worker, as a passage from *Capital,* Vol. I points out:

> The product is the property of the capitalist and not that of the laborer, its immediate producer. Suppose that a capitalist pays for a day's labor-power at its value; then the right to use that power for a day belongs to him, just as much as the right to any other commodity, such as a horse that he has hired for the day. To the purchaser of a commodity belongs its use, and the seller of labor-power, by giving his labor does no more, in reality, than part with the use-value that he has sold. From the instant he steps into the workshop, the use-value of his labor-power, and therefore also its use, which is labor, belongs to the capitalist. By the purchase of labor-power, the capitalist incorporates labor, as a living ferment, with lifeless constituents of the product. . . . The product of this process belongs, therefore, to him, just as much as does the wine

which is the product of a process of fermentation completed in his cellar. . . . The circumstance, that on the one hand the daily sustenance of labor-power costs only half a day's labor, while on the other hand the very same labor-power can work during a whole day, that consequently the value which its use during one day creates, is double what he pays for that use, this circumstance is, without a doubt, a piece of luck for the buyer, but by no means an injury to the seller.[34]

Referring to this and similar passages Richard Miller writes:

In sum, a wage bargain is an equal exchange if the wage embodies or commands the social labor needed to maintain the worker for the period in question. And Marx takes pains to show that this amount of labor will typically be less than the labor expended under the wage bargain. . . .

Marx certainly thought that any system in which production depends on wage bargains resulting in surplus value would eventually generate widespread servitude and suffering. Such were his reasons for being against all economic systems of this kind. This is a very different indictment from the charge that systems depending on surplus value should be condemned because surplus value violates a right to equal exchange.[35]

If Marx did not condemn capitalism for its unjust distribution of social goods or for a violation of a right to equal exchange in the wage bargain, he nevertheless appears to condemn capitalism for its infringement of workers' rights to dignity and freedom. Although later in this chapter I will argue that Marx does indeed morally condemn capitalism for its infringement of human freedom, Marx does not base his criticism on a conception of rights. Marx, I will argue, believed all rights-based claims for equality to be inherently faulty. He argued that whenever a single rights-based claim is set forth, another equally valid but opposing right can be identified. For example, parents' rights to direct and control the curricula for their children frequently conflict with the community's right to make decisions pertaining to children's eduction. An individual student's right to pursue his or her own educational interests without interference conflicts with the rights of others to a fair distribution of educational goods and burdens. Marx viewed this conflict between rights as an inherent aspect of all rights-based claims. And as Miller points out:

> Marx's specific and explicit arguments continue the case saying that every right is a right of inequality. They are meant to show that no right which his contemporaries had advanced was preeminent enough to resolve conflicts without encountering a contrary, equally basic right. That the general problem had not been resolved even approximately, despite centuries of trying, made it a good bet, by Marx's time, that it was insoluble.[36]

Marx did not condemn capitalism for an inequitable distribution of social goods, a violation of rights to equal exchange, or as an infringement of basic human rights. For Marx all of these standards were faulty. Justice, it seems, was not a standard to which Marx appealed. And yet, given Marx's proclivity to make seemingly moral assessments condemning capitalism, the original question still stands: What is the basis for this condemnation? The basis exists, I believe, in Marx's notion of freedom.

Marx's naturalist ethic and the principle of freedom

In contrast to Wood's anti-moral interpretation, other writers view Marx as condemning capitalism on explicitly moral grounds. Although these interpretations vary, the essential claim is that Marx criticized capitalism because it frustrates the satisfaction of basic human needs and inhibits the flourishing of human potential. Marx, the argument proceeds, believed this frustration and inhibition constitutes a moral transgression. Marx's ethic is a naturalist ethic. Men and women have certain basic physical and emotional needs (e.g., food, shelter, and security) and as human beings are defined by certain essential capacities (e.g., a projective self consciousness and self determination). Norman Geras outlines the rationale of a naturalist ethic when he states that

. . . an ethical position resting upon a conception of human
nature is a perfectly possible one, possible in the sense of
being logically unobjectionable, coherent in principle. If one
places a value upon human life and human happiness and
there exist universal needs that must be satisfied respectively
to preserve and promote these, then this furnishes the value
and the fact conjointly, a basis for normative judgments; such
needs ought to be satisfied . . .[37]

Geras and John McMurtry have argued for this naturalist reading
as the correct interpretation of Marx's judgement, as a basis of a
properly conceived Marxist social theory, and against the view of
a morally value-free Marxist framework. George Brenkert extends
and develops the argument, maintaining that Marx's assessment is
based on a naturalist ethic whose major criterion is freedom.

Whether one reads Marx's condemnation as moral or nonmoral,
most commentators agree that Marx viewed exploitation negatively. Exploitation, as Nancy Holstrom succinctly defines it, resides
in the "fact that the [capitalist's] income is derived through forced,
unpaid, surplus [wage] labor, the product of which the workers
do not control."[38] What distinguishes a moral from a nonmoral
reading is whether a situation in which workers are forced to
contribute their unpaid labor is viewed as a transgression of moral
or rational values. As indicated earlier, Wood interprets the lack of
freedom as a violation of rational, not moral criteria. For Wood the
ethical domain is limited to edicts of conscience or "natural law,"
the realm of duty and obligation. Exploitation is a restriction of an
individual's freedom, but since one cannot be "obliged" to be free,
curtailments of freedom cannot constitute moral transgressions.
Brenkert views this definition of the moral as too narrow.

Discussion of Marx's moral views has hitherto been deficient
because it has failed to recognize a common distinction
between two different conceptions of morality. . . . We
must recognize, that is, that the notion of morality is
not a simple and unambiguous notion. We must distinguish
between an ethics of duty and an ethics of virtue. On the
one hand, morality has been viewed as centrally concerned
with the duties and obligations one person owes to another.
So viewed morality is characterized by certain notions such

as duty, obligation, guilt, rights, etc. On this understanding of morality, to be moral is to act in accordance with certain moral laws and duties, or to be moved by a sense of moral obligation. . . . If one then assumes that this view is the only (proper) view of morality, one will quite naturally conclude that Marx must have been a scientist. . . .

However, there is another understanding of morality which should not be forgotten. This is the sense of morality in which morality is linked with certain virtues, excellences or flourishing ways of living. In this sense, morality is not primarily concerned with rules and principles but with the cultivation of certain dispositions or traits of character.[39]

Employing this distinction between an ethic of duty and one of virtue, Brenkert argues that Marx's condemnation was a moral critique rooted in an ethic of virtue. According to Brenkert, Marx was a critic of an ethic of duty, which includes the standard of justice, but rested his moral critique of capitalism and his future vision of communism on an ethic of virtue. Based on this notion of an ethic of virtue and on exegetical evidence, Brenkert contends that Marx's basis for critique is a standard of freedom, an ethic that encourages the full flourishing of the human potential. While Brenkert stresses the role of freedom in Marx's naturalist ethic, I would include, and I do not think Brenkert would disagree substantially, additional human and social goods in Marx's naturalist ethic. In order to achieve the full realization of the human potential, it would seem that human reciprocity and the avoidance of human suffering and degradation are also important. For the remainder of this chapter I will highlight, as Brenkert does, the role of freedom in Marx's ethics, for its appears that freedom is a central value in his ethical stance and the one he uses to condemn capitalism.

Marx's notion of freedom is not solely defined negatively, as the absence of social coercion, but also positively as "a life of self-development within rational and harmonious relations to others."[40] As Brenkert puts it, Marx's concept of freedom "is for one to live such that one essentially determines, within communal relations to other people, the concrete totality of desires, capacities and talents which constitute one's self-objectification."[41] There are three interrelated aspects of this notion of freedom. First, in order for men and women to achieve self determination they must identify (objectify) their own desires, capacities, and talents. Second, in order to recognize and develop adequately these desires, capacities, and talents, individuals must "concretely" realize these personal attributes, and this can only occur when people act in and on the social and natural world to transform it in accordance with their personal characters. (This is called "self objectification.") Finally, according to Brenkert "self determination is only possible within harmonious communal relations,"[42] and thus, the self determination of all is only possible within a system of cooperative social relations.

So as to lend further credence to Marx's concept of freedom and also point out its difficulties, I will discuss briefly these three propositions. I will discuss, however, only the bare essentials. Since the claim of this chapter is not that Marx provides an irrefutable or ultimately persuasive ethical foundation, but rather that Marx presumed and a Marxist social theory entails some sort of moral criteria, such bare essentials are all that is needed.

The meaning of the first proposition, that in order to become self determining one must identify his or her own desires, capacities, and talents, is not particularly troublesome. To be able to direct one's own life requires that one know what one is capable of and desires. Self determination without a knowledge of one's desires and talents cannot be *self* determination. But which desires and talents are conducive to self determination? If one desires to spend an inordinate amount of time watching the waves lapping the ocean shore, does acting on this desire constitute an act of self determination? Brenkert thinks it implausible, within a Marxist ethic, to call such a person free: "In certain circumstances our desires may become fetters on us, powers over us."[43] When a single desire becomes rigid and does not allow the fulfillment of a "totality of desires, capacities and talents," self determination is inhibited. Brenkert, however, admits that the fulfillment of an individual's "totality" of desires is "silly." Some desires conflict, and others require more time and energy to develop fruitfully. If a rigid adherence to actions based on particular desires fetters self development and acting on all desires is simply unfeasible, one looks for general guidelines to indicate the possibilities for self development. Brenkert believes Marx provides such guidelines, but a close inspection of Brenkert's text does not reveal any formulation. While this lacuna does point to an insufficiency in an elaboration of Marx's notion of freedom, it seems, in principle at least, capable of resolution.[44]

Another obstacle to the identification and development of one's desires, capabilities, and talent lies in an incorrect understanding of how society works. Self determination entails a recognition of which natural and social relations are and which are not amenable to human alteration and direction. All too often this recognition is obscured. Accordingly Brenkert notes that

> . . . self determination implies a knowledge and understand-
> ing of one's life conditions and relations, how they arose and
> how they operate . . . . self determination involves individual
> control of one's affairs in light of a rational understanding
> of the situation in which ones lives and the nature of the
> processes underlying that situation. Those who live under
> capitalism may believe that they are self-determining and
> free, but in reality they are not. This is true not only of the
> proletarian but also the capitalist.[45]

The second proposition may be more obscure than the first. The essential idea behind Marx's notion of self objectification is that humans only come to know who they are through acting in and on the social and natural world. Through acts of transformative labor an individual objectifies and comes to know himself or herself.[46] This does not strike me as an exceptionally controversial or troubling notion. It may be contested that self objectification is not the only or most efficacious route to the recognition and development of an individual's desires, capacities, and talents. Self knowledge arises from introspection, where little if any transformative action occurs. But it seems that Marx and Brenkert would argue that the development of one's capacities and talents necessarily requires action in the real world and not mere contemplation.

Furthermore, not any type of transformative activity suffices. Marx's position is that it is necessary for the individual to relate to nature and other people in terms of "concrete and individual qualities" and not in terms of "abstract, universal powers." It is only when people approach each other as fellow beings with similar needs, interests, desires, and capacities that "real human" bonds will develop. And it is only when these bonds are developed that truly transformative activity can occur. In the absence of "concrete" bonds, abstract bonds develop that separate rather than join individuals together and destroy the possibility of transformative action. As Brenkert writes:

> Marx's position is that the one who mediately objectifies himself by abstract powers does not have to develop his own qualities, as required by the object of his will. Instead universal and abstract power (e.g. money) is invoked which eliminates the need for one's actions and relations to be bound to one's individuality or take cognizance of the specific nature of the other person. In that situation, I am like the master in Hegel's master-slave dialectic. I do not essentially experience the realization or objectification of myself. Rather I know the realization of something else. There is no longer self determination, but other-determination of the self.[47]

In capitalism neither capitalists nor workers are able to objectify themselves.

The third aspect of Marx's conception of freedom, the necessity of communal relations, does not further define Marx's notion of freedom but rather stipulates that communal social relations are a necessary condition for the exercise of a fully developed sense of freedom. The community makes possible the exercise of self determination. Brenkert's elaboration of the Marxist conception of community takes many detours, but for my purposes it is essential to note two characteristics. In a Marxian community there would be a harmonization of the members' essential interests. Since Marx views human productive labor as the arena for self determination, it is essential that any antagonistic interests in the productive sphere (class divisions) be replaced with a recognition of shared concerns. Second, the community would be characterized by human interaction on the basis of concrete qualities, not abstract powers. Production would be based on use value not exchange value. When the essential antagonism of interests no longer exists to divide and separate people and when individuals recognize the shared human interests and relate concretely, then the foundation for individual self determination exists. As Brenkert notes:

> Marx held that if there did not exist antagonistic interests at the basis of society, there would be a ripple effect on

the rest of society. On the one hand, the personal relations amongst individuals would be changed. If one's labor does not set one off against others, make one feel threatened by others, then one's relations with others will be themselves more harmonious. There will be an overcoming of bourgeois society's predominant concern with self interest, i.e. its concern with others only to the extent that they fulfill a person's own ends. In this sense, the harmony of basic interests not only itself constitutes but fosters a broader and deeper identification of an individual with others.[48]

If Marx's notion of freedom translates roughly into a recognition and development of an individual's desires, capacities, and talents through self objectification, then Marx's argument for the necessity of a community is as follows. It is only in a community, within communal social relations, that individuals can recognize their desires and capacities and that self objectification can occur. In a community people will treat each other concretely, they will identify with others, and they will not be separated from each other. Under these conditions, Marx believed, people are able to engage in transformative labor and action in the world that objectifies and develops their talents, capacities and desires. In any other situation human labor will not be a transformation and objectification of individuals' true desires but rather a realization of the antagonism that separates them.

Conclusion

The criterion for Marx's condemnation of capitalism appears to be a standard of freedom, a standard that is contained within a naturalist ethic. Human beings are such that in order to be human they must be free. If men and women's freedom is restricted, if servitude rather than freedom prevails, then humanity is denigrated. Marx thought capitalism denigrates the lives of a majority if not all of the men and women living under it. In essence capitalism is the source of human servitude.

In Marx's view, freedom, not justice or equality, serves as the central ethical standard on which capitalism was critiqued and condemned. As noted in the beginning of this chapter, recent Marxists criticize capitalism and schooling in capitalism as a form of servitude *and* inequality. If the argument presented here is sufficiently persuasive, the implications should be fairly apparent. Marx believed critiques based on the notions of equality, equal rights, and justice to be either misdirected or seriously inadequate. Today, Marxists who employ the standards of justice or equality must at least recognize and appraise the merits of Marx's own critique of these standards and either revise the basis of their critiques or argue against Marx's position. It can no longer be assumed that a Marxist approach to schooling and society condemns the inequalities or injustices of a capitalist society. Current theorists can, no doubt, disagree with Marx's formulation, but the disagreement must be recognized and attempts made to rectify the incongruity.

I will assume, as it seems a sound assumption, that freedom was and still remains the central ethical standard for Marxist critiques. Given this assumption, it is now incumbent on those working in the Marxist tradition to examine the standard of freedom's capacity to justify educational changes. Marxists frequently celebrate the notion of praxis, a concept that hints at the unification of thought and practice. Marxist analyses of schools are not intended as simply formal exercises in the analysis and evaluation of schooling but as necessary preparatory studies prior to and in conjunction with social and political action. If capitalism and schooling are to be condemned because of the servitude they inflict, then it seems reasonable to assume that the actions taken enhance, rather than detract from, the potentiality for freedom. The next chapter shall address the difficulties attending this issue.

6

Ethical values and
Marxist educational prescriptions

Marxists criticize schools for unnecessarily restricting students' freedom and explain how schools accomplish this restriction, yet they do envision schools as places where the development of freedom is a reasonable and feasible goal. Such visions encounter not only practical but also intellectual difficulties. So far, radicals have not sufficiently confronted the intellectual and ethical problems that attend their calls for educational action. They have neither scrutinized their own prescriptions nor provided substantial justifications for their educational agendas. In this chapter I will examine the intellectual tasks involved in prescribing and justifying Marxist educational programs. Specifically I will focus on three general areas: 1) an examination of the procedures available to justify educational programs; 2) a comparison of two socialist educational programs that recognize the Marxist concern for freedom; and 3) an exploration of a few key problems posed by the Marxist conception of freedom when applied to public schooling. As a result of this analysis the scope and direction of Marxist educational prescriptions should become clearer and a few of the central difficulties should come to light.

First, though, a prior issue needs to be confronted. If the Marxist theory of public education has as one of its goals the development of free individuals and the transformation of capitalism, then the role of public schools in societal change needs to be delineated. Only if schools can contribute to changes in society does it seem reasonable to support educational action for social change. There are least three ways to construe the role of schools in societal trans-formations: 1) as reflective of and determined by the larger society;

2) as central and determinant institutions in the transformation of society; or 3) as capable of supporting but not directing social transformations. Historically, all three views have been adopted, at various times, by the political left. It appears, though, that the third alternative most realistically portrays schools' role in societal transformations and is also consistent with much of the recent radical work.

The first interpretation states that in a capitalist society schools will be "capitalist" schools. Usually this view is characterized as the classical materialist and determinist interpretation of the school-society linkage. Accordingly, if the societal context changes, then schools will change, but otherwise schools will remain essentially as they are. Recently critics have argued that this interpretation belittles the potential of human agency and is theoretically reductive and empirically incorrect. Critics argue that once schools are construed as determined by larger social forces, the possibility for political action is negated, hope is lost, and educational work devalued.[1] Other writers argue that while schools are constrained and limited by the social forces in capitalism, they are not determined in any strict sense by either the economic or political demands of a capitalist society. Here the recent Marxist work on culture and the state becomes important. Much of this recent analysis argues that state institutions (e.g., public schools) maintain an important degree of autonomy from the economic demands of society and that the cultural meaning people create and maintain is not determined by the capitalist mode of production.[2] Although there are some Marxists who would maintain that the determinist reading of schools captures best the relations between schools and society, recent work does not support that view.

The second interpretation of the school-society linkage places educational institutions at the vanguard of social transformations. This outlook has been supported by Progressive American educators after the Great Depression and more recently by a few of the educators involved in the 1960s radical school movement.[3] It seems, however, that this view entails a flight of fancy from the real world of schooling. It expects children eventually to transform what adults have not. This view is not supported by the historical record but rather seems to be sustained by a faith and hope we hold for our children's future. There is little reason to suppose, however, that Marx viewed schools as central to the transformation of capitalism. While one might argue that Marx viewed education as an important element in the struggle for socialism, it would be difficult to interpret Marx's few comments about public schooling as an indication that schools could serve as an arena for vanguard action. Marx's criticisms of the emphasis John Owen placed on educational reform reinforces this interpretation.[4]

The third option, that schools cannot direct but can support social transformations, gains credence as a result of the other two interpretations' frailties, but positive arguments are also available. Education transforms individuals' cognitive abilities and alters their understandings of the world. In order for class action to occur, individuals would have to be willing and able to take the necessary social and political actions. Schools cannot direct this class activity, but they can either inadequately or adequately provide students with the cognitive abilities and general knowledge needed for successful class action. Historically, Marx viewed public education not as an insignificant factor in the struggle for socialism.[5] He believed that an ignorant population was more easily mystified and misled than an educated one. Further support for this interpretation is possible but it would require more attention than I am willing to give. Suffice it to say that within the Marxist framework, educational arrangements, while certainly no antidote for the degradation resulting from capitalism, can contribute to its transformation.

The justification of educational programs

If schools can contribute to the transformation of capitalism, then it does not seem unreasonable to construct educational agendas for social change. Marxists have identified educational programs but have paid little attention to how the Marxist premise of freedom justifies or guides their educational programs.[6] Marxists are rather quick to point to the degradations brought about by capitalism and schooling in capitalist society but rarely do they attend to the moral basis or implications of their own programs. Although some ethical analysis does exist, it is for the most part infrequent and not sustained.[7] Rather than provide ethical justifications for their acclaimed alternatives, Marxists tend to justify their programs through an appeal to the social and political "facts." Marxists characterize schooling in capitalism as pernicious, identify the links between capitalism and schooling, and then launch into prescriptions for curricular and pedagogical change. This approach can be found in the analyses of both Henry Giroux and Jean Anyon.

Giroux proposes a plan for radical pedagogy and constructs a justification for this program through a description of the dialectics of social change.[8] Reacting to deterministic or reductionist theories of social change, Giroux asserts that the world changes "dialectically," an assessment that is for Giroux a source of hope. If the explanation of social change is deterministic there is no hope.[9] This inference from an empirical assertion to an optative sentiment forms the ultimate basis for Giroux's proposal for a radical pedagogy, a pedagogy that "educates" politically radical activists. With this hope in hand, we can now see schools as an active force in the dialectic of social change and radical pedagogy as a tool for emancipation. The justification for this program of radical pedagogy is an empirical assertion about social change. It seems that Giroux's argument is lacking essential ethical justification. "Educating" radical activists in the public schools cannot be justified by a notion of dialectical social change.

Anyon elaborates a theoretical model of "non-reproductive" education. According to Anyon, this model "incorporates notions of contradictory or dual social consciousness, a dialectical view of social change and a set of situated (class-specific), transformative pedagogies."[10] Similar to Giroux's approach, Anyon's justification for educational activity ignores the ethical dimension. It assumes that if people's social consciousness is contradictory and the process of social change is dialectical, then certain pedagogical interventions are "justified." She writes

> It seems to me that we are today at a particular historical
> juncture in which the dialectic between cultural activity
> and economic change is particularly acute. Capitalism is
> becoming increasingly unmanageable and increasingly diffi-
> cult to rationalize ideologically. Because of the material and
> legitimation crises, popular ideological equivocation or oppo-
> sition is likely. Rejection can take many forms however. . . .
> It is within this possibility of radically different alternatives

that appropriate politicized cultural work is needed—to make a crucial difference. One way that educators can make a contribution to such work is through a socially-situated, class-specific, politicizing education.[11]

A class-specific, political education is justified by the claim of an acute, emerging contradiction between the cultural and economic spheres of society. Anyon employs an interpretation of societal change to justify her educational program.

Both Giroux and Anyon prescribe educational programs. They suggest to others what educational actions ought to be taken. In order to justify an educational prescription, one must consider its ethical implications. In effect, it is incumbent on these authors to tell us why we ought to engage in a plan of "radical pedagogy" or a "class-specific educational program." Talk about the social, political, or economic realities of schooling does not provide the ethical reasoning necessary to justify radical or class-based educational programs. Descriptions of schools and their curricula or explanations linking schools to capitalism cannot justify programs of educational and political action. Empirical appraisals may indicate that specific actions are likely or unlikely to generate particular consequences, but such empirical assessments cannot provide the moral legitimacy for proposed educational programs. In order to justify educational activities one must begin to assess a program's goals and the means proposed to achieve those goals.

Giroux and Anyon do not provide substantial justifications for their educational proposals. One could argue that it is neither Giroux nor Anyon's task ethically to justify their educational programs. Their task is simply to provide and describe additional educational avenues, and they achieve that goal. There may be some truth to this response, but it should be evident that such justifications are sorely needed.

It might be argued that Marx's naturalist ethic provides the basis for the justification of radical educational proposals. The naturalist premise conjoins factual and evaluative elements when it states that since people are human only when they are free, people ought to be free, and accordingly furnishes the ethical foundation for radical educational programs. But such a claim miscontrues the scope of this "synthesis" of fact and value. While

Marx's naturalist ethic grounds the Marxist value for freedom and the subsequent condemnation of capitalism, this naturalist ethic cannot identify which actions are freedom producing or which actions enable the flourishing of the human potential, nor does it outline a general procedure to distinguish which actions ought to be pursued. The Marxist naturalist premise cannot be extended to a generalized proposition that states that "facts justify human choices." The naturalist premise is specific to and justifies only the Marxist value for freedom. Even with a naturalist ethic in hand, we do not know whether 1) we intuit which curricular proposals are freedom developing courses of action; 2) we measure the probable consequences of certain educational programs and thereby determine which proposal to follow; or 3) we believe that certain educational activities are intrinsically related to concerns for freedom and should be undertaken regardless of the consequences. In short, the naturalist premise furnishes the foundation for the value of freedom but not a general procedure for deciding which educational actions and designs are most promising.

If one turns to Marx's own writings or the secondary literature on Marx and ethics to discern what ethical procedures are contained within or are compatible with a Marxist framework, little agreement is found. While it appears evident to most that Marx condemned capitalism for its restriction of freedom, it is not clear whether or how Marx justified his appeals for political and social action. Some argue that Marx did not but should have offered a justification and point to Marx's inconsistencies.[12] Others argue that Marx's ethical justification employs a utilitarian procedure such that Marx justified political action to the degree that it hastened the arrival of socialism, thereby providing the greatest amount of satisfaction.[13] Still others argue that Marx was a non-utilitarian consequentialist who utilized a number of distinct criteria to assess the consequences of various actions. The merits of each interpretation cannot be assessed here. Instead I will present, as the most plausible view, Richard Miller's interpretation of Marx as a non-utilitarian consequentialist. Miller's reading seems to represent best Marx's own argument and also appears to capture one manner in which everyday decisions are made and justified. Here I want only to portray Miller's reading as a very plausible interpretation of Marx's ethical procedure, one that can be utilized by educational theorists and practitioners in the critical tradition.[14]

A non-utilitarian consequentialist procedure

Miller's portrayal of Marx's logic of justification involves at least four distinct components: 1) actions and institutional arrangements are assessed with regard to their probable consequences; 2) a diversity of social goods and goals are employed as criteria to assess the probable consequences; 3) a particular rational procedure is used to mediate between the abstract goals and the concrete social and political choices; and 4) a sociology of desired human traits, institutional features, and social goals is outlined. Marx's emphasis on the probable consequences of human actions and institutional arrangements has been characterized by Miller as a non-utilitarian consequentialist procedure. According to Miller, Marx employs a procedure that assesses the consequences of actions or institutional arrangements according to the kind of human life they would encourage. In a strictly utilitarian calculation actions and social arrangements are judged appropriate if their consequences enhance the total welfare of the population, with welfare "regarded as a sum of mental phenomena . . . measured in a scientific and non-evaluative manner."[15] In a utilitarian framework educational arrangements and pedagogical actions would be justified if they contribute positively toward the happiness and satisfaction of those involved.[16] Marx, however, criticized the utilitarian "philosophy of enjoyment" in both the *German Ideology* and *Capital*, arguing that its narrow focus distorted the human potential by reducing the wealth of all human endeavors to the value of enjoyment.[17] In Miller's interpretation Marx does not assess institutions by a criterion of welfare (or pleasure) but instead judges them by the kinds of lives they promote,[18] by the kinds of human beings they encourage to flourish. Marx's consequentialism differs from a utilitarian assessment in that Marx recognizes a plurality and irreducible diversity of human goods and social goods. Freedom (and its corresponding notions), human reciprocity, and the avoidance of human suffering and degradation are among the general goods Marx values.[19]

It is important to identify the probable consequences of human actions and institutional arrangements in Marx's ethical procedure and then to assess the degree to which such actions and arrangements facilitate the achievement of the desired goals and goods. Frequently, though, there is difficulty in identifying the probable consequences of human actions and institutional features and in assessing the degree to which these consequences are conducive to the desired goods and goals. According to Miller's reading, Marx's justificatory logic minimizes these difficulties by utilizing 1) a rational procedure relating particular choices to abstract goals, and 2) a sociology that loosely connects particular human traits, institutional features, and desired goods. Miller elaborates Marx's justificatory logic connecting the particular to the general and hints at the sociology of traits and features when he writes:

> Marx's social choices are supposed to be justified among
> those concerned with freedom, reciprocity, the avoidance
> of suffering and other goods, if the emphases they place
> on different aspects of these goods are sufficient to support
> the choice of socialism. This circularity is not to be removed
> by a more careful definition of the required emphases. It
> corresponds to the logic of justification, here. People con-
> cerned in general with freedom, reciprocity, the avoidance
> of suffering and other familiar goals are presented with an
> empirical argument about the inevitable consequences of
> capitalism and the possibilities for change under socialism.
> If they accept those arguments and respond with a basic
> social choice, it is usually a choice of socialism. That choice
> further defines their underlying goals. In an epistemologi-
> cal turn characteristic of both Marx and Hegal, rational
> people move from the general (the abstract goals) to the
> particular (the grasp of actual social consequences) and
> back to a revision of the general (the further specification
> of goals).[20]

The difficulty entailed in mediating between general and abstract values and the choices available in the concrete social world is partially resolved by this deliberative process. In addition to this model of deliberation, Miller points out that Marx provides a sociology that links desired human traits with certain institutional features and connects these traits and features to a catalog of desired goods. As Miller explains, Marx presents

> . . . a hierarchy of independent but related recommendations, passing from a catalog of general human goods to a description of social arrangements to be pursued, to a description of the workers' movement that achieves them, to a sketch of the character traits that motivate individual choices. A lower-lever standard is partly but not wholly determined by the next highest. Most, but not all, rational people who are committed to the higher-level choice will be led to make the lower-level choice if they accept Marx's evidence and social theories. Similarly, the higher, more general standards eliminate some, but not all, rivals to the lower, more specific ones. Someone committed to the general catalog will not choose the elitist goals of a Nietzche, but might, in principle, opt for a form of capitalist democracy. Someone who regards a Marxist workers' movement as desirable could not coherently lead the life of a Christian evangelist. But he or she might stay on the sidelines, wishing the movement well without taking part.[21]

This sociological linkage is not a tight, preprogrammed agenda but rather a loose empirical assessment of the type of character traits, political movements, and societal arrangements that would tend to promote the desired goals.

According to Miller, Marx's justificatory schema identifies the desired goods and goals, assesses actions and institutions according to their ability to contribute toward these goals, employs a rational deliberative process to mediate between the abstract goals and concrete available choices, and finally provides a sociology of traits and features that would facilitate the accomplishment of these goals. Two characteristics of this ethical procedure stand out: 1) its emphasis on consequences contributes to a justificatory procedure that is contextually dependent, and 2) the stress on consequences tends toward an extreme form of instrumentalism, one in which violent means may be justified in order to achieve desired ends or indoctrinatory approaches may be supported. Both of these features require further discussion before moving onto an analysis of two socialist educational programs.

Miller emphasizes that Marx's justificatory procedure does not predetermine specific actions or institutional features as *the* singular route to the achievement of human freedom. Both Marx's deliberative model and his sociology of traits and features underline the need for flexibility when justifying social and political choices. The deliberative model, in which decisions are perceived as the outcome of a mediation between general goals and concrete options, leaves plenty of room for a diverse set of outcomes. Marx's loose linking of human traits, institutional features, and desired goals, while providing some direction in this deliberative process, is nevertheless quite flexible. If one accepts the basic good of human freedom, then Marx presents socialism as the social formation most conducive to meeting that goal, solidarity in activism as the reasonable means to achieve socialism, and compassion and risk taking as human traits conducive to the collective struggle. This "sociology" provides a skeletal outline of the empirical route toward freedom, but within that sketch many options are open.

This flexibility has implications for proposed educational programs. The specification of pedagogical actions, curricular options, and institutional arrangements conducive to the Marxist goal of freedom are highly dependent on the social and political context, or the "facts" of the situation. Whenever and wherever the facts substantially differ, so, it would seem, would the Marxist educational prescription. Paulo Freire's emancipatory educational proposals for the oppressed peoples of the third world may be justified in their contexts but not in other settings.[22] The Bolshevik Anton Makarenko's militaristic educational practices may have been justified following the Russian Revolution.[23] I point to these two examples not to make the case that they are justified but rather to illustrate the possibility of potentially justifiable and diverse socialist educational programs. Given that Marx's justificatory procedure is tied to the consequences of actions and arrangements in specific settings, it would not be surprising to find dissimilar educational proposals appropriately entitled "Marxist."

This reliance on the assessment of consequences in factually diverse situations points to another facet of a Marxist justification. As outlined here, the Marxist ethical procedure is very dependent on appraisals of social and political realities. Abstract goals are redefined in light of the available empirical options, and the sociology of institutional features and human traits acts as a guide in the justification and choice of alternative courses of action. Explanatory sketches and investigations are a necessary feature of Marxist programmatic efforts. In order to assess the probable consequences of an educational arrangement, one must be acquainted with the social, political, and economic realities of capitalism. The Marxist pursuit of human freedom requires a clear understanding and explanation of the social and natural worlds. In order to become self determining, one must know which social relations are amenable to human transformation. In education this implies that the curriculum must contain empirically accurate explanations of capitalism. For students to become self determining, the realities of capitalism must be unveiled.

Miller's consequentialist reading of Marx's justificatory procedure also raises a distinctly moral concern. Employing this procedure, it appears possible for one to justify a wide variety of means as long as they achieve the desired end. Marxism, on the extreme reading, cares most for the eventual destruction of capitalism and the triumph of socialism. If violent means achieve the desired goals, then violent action (against perceived violent conditions) may well be justified. This view tends toward an excessive and, at times, violent form of instrumentalism.[24]

Within Marxist educational proposals this instrumentalism does not take the violent form noted above but instead appears in goals of "educating" radicals or instituting class-based pedagogies.[25] In these educational proposals class-based activists and radicals are seen as necessary for and instrumental to social transformations, and the public school's task is to "educate" these activists. Such agendas raise the specter of indoctrination. Schools are to produce students with particular beliefs, political values, and cognitive views of the world. As an educator I find such proposals unacceptable. If the Marxist justificatory schema entails, condones, or supports such an instrumental view, I would argue that the schema would have to be drastically revised or totally rejected. However, a number of authors writing in the Marxist tradition raise substantial objections to this extreme form of instrumentalism. Richard Miller, George Brenkert, and Richard Norman provide distinct reasons for rejecting this instrumentalist interpretation.

Miller argues that a purely instrumental reading of Marx is "implausible."

> In the best reconstruction of his arguments, Marx is recommending his conception of the workers' movement both as something that effectively creates socialism, and as something with positive value in the context of capitalism. Both features play an important, indispensable role. . . .
>   Marx, though he sometimes justifies workers' violence that the press condemns, never appeals to the consideration that everything is excused if it contributes to socialism. He seems to have shared in the general rejection of extreme instrumentalism.[26]

This view of Marx as a tempered instrumentalist is shared by Brenkert, who argues that for Marx violent means are justified "when the following conjoint conditions are satisfied: a) they would be efficacious in bringing about communism; b) other peaceful, open, and/or honest means are unavailable or prohibited."[27] Marx does not license violent action but views it as a possible course if other means are unavailable.

Norman notes that it is frequently argued that if a socialist society can be brought into existence by means that run counter to the Marxist view of freedom, either by means of repression, exploitation, or elitism, such actions are sanctioned. Their justification lies in an exchange of short-term losses for long-term gains. The short-term injuries caused by such repressive means would, supposedly, be recouped by the long-term achievement of a socialist society. For Norman, however, there is another important consideration.

> . . . someone for whom the Marxist ethic is not just a commitment to a certain ideal of human society but a commitment to a certain kind of life might look at the matter differently. He might say that to use such methods would be to go against everything he stands for and everything to which he is committed. He might perhaps express it by saying that, even if such action offers a greater chance of success, he could never bring himself to do it. What stands in the way is the kind of life he is committed to, the way in which he is committed

to it, and the way in which this kind of commitment gives his life its point. From this point of view, it is perfectly rational to assert that one has no choice but to commit oneself to revolutionary action while accepting the fact that it may offer a lesser chance of success.[28]

These three authors temper the instrumentalism inherent in the consequentialist approach. It seems clear that this tendency toward instrumentalism exists and should be recognized by those utilizing the framework, and unless the tendency is recognized, the radical route to freedom may be more pernicious than the very serious injuries of capitalism.

Thus far I have examined what I consider to be the most promising and consistent interpretation of a Marxist justificatory schema, an approach that employs a consequentialist procedure, assesses human actions and institutional arrangements according to whether they contribute to a diverse range of human goods and social goods, mediates between concrete options and abstract and general goods, and relies, to some degree, on a sociology of human traits, institutional features, and desired goods. I have argued that Marxist educational proposals are contextually dependent and therefore limited by what is feasible. However, Marxist educational proposals are also limited by the concern for freedom. In order to understand some of the substantive features of a distinctively Marxist approach to education, I will now move on to a brief discussion and comparison of two socialist educational proposals.

Two socialist educational agendas

I want to analyze briefly two educational programs that recognize the Marxist concern for freedom. As a part of this analysis, I will identify the salient features of Marxist educational agendas and highlight a few of the conceptual difficulties involved in these agendas. Since the Marxist justificatory procedure is contextually dependent, Marxism cannot present one route as the educational avenue to freedom. The Marxist commitment to freedom cannot stipulate a single educational program, but it does limit the educational options and also directs attention toward particular concerns. These options and concerns can be noted by briefly re-examining the conception of freedom outlined in the previous chapter.[29]

In Chapter 5 I indicated that the Marxist notion of freedom contained three interrelated aspects. First, in order to achieve self determination, men and women must identify their desires, capacities, and talents and also know which natural and social relations are amenable to human alteration. Second, individuals must concretely realize their personal attributes, which can only occur when people act in and on their social and natural world to transform it in accordance with their personal characters. Finally, as Brenkert puts it, "self-determination is only possible within harmonious communal relations,"[30] and thus, the self determination of all is only possible within a system of cooperative social relations. In their respective educational programs Stephen Castles and Wibke Wustenberg, and David Reynolds and Michael Sullivan recognize the Marxist concern for freedom but each approach it differently.[31]

Castles and Wustenberg attempt to delineate the kind of education conducive to the "emancipation of the suppressed and exploited classes."[32] They argue that the

> . . . core of Marxist theory is the idea of the development
> of a new type of human being; the "totally developed
> individual" who is capable of controlling a rational process
> of production and distribution within a new form of society
> —"an association of free men." Work—the struggle of man
> with nature in order to satisfy his needs—is, for Marx,
> the specifically human activity which is vital for the
> self-realisation of man.[33]

With the goal of developed, free and self-realized human beings, Castles and Wustenberg maintain that the most significant element in their educational program is the curriculum.

> The foremost principle of education for social transformation
> is that it must help people to understand the world they live
> in. This refers to the natural world—the material conditions
> and scientific laws which form the basis of production—and to

the social world—the economic, social and political structures of society.[34]

If people understand the natural and social world, they will be able to identify, and be that much closer to transforming, those aspects amenable to human control. Capitalism can therefore be understood, challenged, and transformed.

In addition to this cognitive emphasis, Castles and Wustenberg underline the importance of work in an educational program. Mental, physical, and technological education should be combined, and in this combination an emphasis should be placed on useful work. Students need to see that work, human transformation, can meet and develop "real human needs and abilities" and that the gulf between public schooling and social and economic problems can be overcome. According to Castles and Wustenberg, "The most important way of doing this is to combine learning with productive work. Taking part in socially necessary production from an early age would help children to understand the real basis of society."[35]

Finally, the authors indicate that the social environment of the school should emphasize collaboration and a sense of community and reduce the emphasis on competition. Pointing to the Tvind Schools in Denmark, they write that "pupils learn to work and to solve problems collectively. Competitiveness is reduced with the realisation that an objective can only be achieved through the ideas and efforts of all participants. Solidarity is regarded as the best precondition for the development of the individual personality."[36] The core elements of Castles and Wustenberg's socialist proposal—the cognitive emphasis, work orientation, and collaborative ethos—characterize a polytechnic educational program, and, as they say,

> . . . the attempt to introduce polytechnic principles and methods in educational work can be a "revolutionary ferment" in a capitalist society. . . . Even though such attempts can only be partially successful, they may still make an important contribution to the struggle against capitalist exploitation and for a new form of society.[37]

In contrast to Castles and Wustenberg's educational proposal, Reynolds and Sullivan argue less for a distinctively socialist approach and more for the maintenance of existing educational arrangements with some socialist modifications. They recognize the emphasis Marx placed on freedom, but argue that an educational program honoring freedom can only occur in a post-capitalist society.

A classical Marxist perspective also, in our opinion, eschews the idea that one of the functions of education in pre-socialist society should be to facilitate the individual learner's freedom to define his own goals and the means to attain those goals. For Marx, the concept of individual goal definition is incompatible with the achievement of goals which are universally beneficial, except in the ultimate communist society in which genuine and free individual development takes place within the context of societal solidarity. In capitalist society, the organization of which promotes individualistic achievement, such freedom to define educational goals and means would act to impede further the growth of that collective political action which is one of the predeterminants (though not the sole predeterminant) of the social and political change from capitalist to socialist society.[38]

According to Reynolds and Sullivan, the probable consequence of an educational program focusing on freedom in a capitalist context is the further fragmentation rather than unification of political action. Rather than focus on goal identification, these authors argue that a "crucial predeterminant of the transformation from capitalism to socialism is the universalization of access to a national education system which retains in its curricular content and pedagogy much that is presently associated with the educational processes of capitalist schooling."[39] For Reynolds and Sullivan universal access to educational provisions is the most important educational strategy toward socialism. However, within their educational program they do emphasize the importance of a basis for secure knowledge of social and natural relations and the need for collective social relations within the school. They argue that "Education in pre-socialist capitalist society should . . . incorporate the rational empiricism of bourgeois culture because such rational empiricism is a prerequisite of a critical awareness of the nature of capitalist society and the subsequent development of a revolutionary theory of practice."[40] They further specify that within the system of public education there should be the "promotion of socialist and co-operative values rather than capitalistic and individualistic values."[41] Essentially Reynolds and Sullivan maintain that schooling in capitalism ought to remain the way it is except that 1) its universalization must be assured; 2) the curriculum must provide a scientific basis for the analysis of social and natural relations; and 3) collectivist and collaborative social relations should be encouraged.

It appears clear that Castles and Wustenberg attempt to build an educational program based on a conception of freedom and that Reynolds and Sullivan, although recognizing the importance of the goal of freedom within the Marxist framework, reject freedom as a basis for their educational agenda. Their differences are, in part, the result of distinct empirical assessments. Reynolds and Sullivan believe that any educational program in a capitalist society that encourages self determination results in the fragmentation of future political action, whereas Castles and Wustenberg argue that any socialist educational agenda in a capitalist society will be only partially successful but that such attempts are also valuable as catalysts for further social and political action. However, the disparity between these two educational programs is not only empirical. Their differences arise from and reveal difficulties in the Marxist conception of freedom. I will briefly examine how this notion of freedom relates to 1) the Marxist commitment to community, 2) a child's natural dependency, and 3) curricula and the problem of indoctrination.

Freedom and education

When applied to the educational context the conception of freedom that involves self determination within communal relations raises a number of concerns that require attention. Given the emphasis on communal relations, it is reasonable to ask to what degree is a communitarian ethos required in order for self determination to occur and lead to a reinforcement rather than a fragmentation of communitarian ties. At issue here is the relationship between the Marxist conceptions of community and self determination.

Reynolds and Sullivan's position is quite clear: Self determination will remain individualistic and fragmented until socialist relations are established. Castles and Wustenberg are not as explicit. They do not address squarely the relationship between self determination and community but do state that a context of solidarity and community provides the best condition for the development of individual personalities. They do not identify the degree of solidarity necessary for this development but it does not seem they would reject all attempts, as do Reynolds and Sullivan. Brenkert outlines an alternative to Reynolds and Sullivan's interpretation. Rather than arguing that collectivist relations must be fully established before engaging in self determination, Brenkert argues:

> Freedom . . . stands in a two fold relation to the community. On the one hand, the community provides each individual with the means of cultivating his gifts in all directions. The community makes possible, in short, the self development of individuals which we saw to be an important part of self-determination. The community, accordingly, stands as a means to the end of individual freedom. . . . On the other hand, life in the community is itself part of the realization of freedom. The communal life is, as such, not simply a means to freedom, but also part of the end, part of freedom, itself.[42]

He adds that "The members of a community jointly participate in the control and direction of the affairs of their community. In doing so they further define and identify the course their interests will take."[43] In Brenkert's reading self determination requires a degree of community, and the community is a result, in part, of efforts at self determination. Thus, it seems that educators need not await a full blown realization of a community ethos but can strive to create a communitarian setting and at the same time engage in the identification and objectification of individuals' desires, capacities, and talents. Here the relationship between self determination and the community is seen as reciprocal and interactive, whereas on Reynolds and Sullivan's interpretation the presence of a collective community is viewed as a necessary condition for self determination.

Additional conceptual difficulties surface if one accepts the educational possibility of self determination through the identification of desires, talents, and capacities. A central issue concerns the conflict between the educational goal of self determination and autonomy *and* the child's natural tendency toward reliance and dependency. Children are biologically and culturally dependent on adults. Some might argue that children are developmentally unsuited for the goal of self determination. Their interests, capacities, and desires are in a state of flux, and they lack the necessary abilities to discern which interests to follow and which capacities to develop. Since the child is not "equipped" to make these decisions, it is the responsibility of the adult, the teacher, to make these decisions. Self determination becomes determination by others, and Marx's definition of freedom is rejected. The problem appears to be whether it is necessary to achieve "adult status" before it is possible to identify and develop one's own interests and desires or whether this "adult status" is the result of earlier attempts at self determination and objectification. This is basically the same issue that arose with the Progressives' emphasis on the child's interests, and it is central to the debates between "child-centered" and "subject-centered" curriculum proposals. I do not intend to resolve the debate. Rather I wish to show that Marxist educational prescriptions based on this notion of freedom must confront questions commonly debated by the educational community. Rather than denigrating issues of conceptual clarification[44] or ignoring shared conundrums, it would seem more profitable for radicals to recognize and attempt to confront these issues.

Finally, I wish to raise an additional concern about Marxism and indoctrination. One of the features of the Marxist concept of freedom is the necessity for accurate knowledge of the social and natural worlds. In order for people to become self determining, they need to know what is amenable to change and how this change occurs. Educationally, this translates into a demand that the curricula accurately depict the natural and social worlds. Castles and Wunstenberg identify an accurate curricula as the basis of their educational program, and Reynolds and Sullivan argue that an accurate curricula lays the groundwork for revolutionary theory. In both proposals there is a heightened concern over curricular content. Now presumably a Marxist would contend that the Marxist framework provides an accurate understanding of the social, political, and economic facets of the human world. But does a Marxist educational agenda support a distinctly Marxist understanding of capitalism or a pluralist offering of social explanatory frameworks? Within the curricula are competing explanatory outlooks offered or is a singular framework preferred? If the Marxist agenda, in its zeal for the "proper" interpretation of the facts, restricts the scope of explanatory frameworks to only those in line with a Marxist reading, then it seems that indoctrination rather than education prevails. Given that Marxist explanations, at least at this time, compete with other frameworks, it would seem empirically premature to proclaim the Marxist framework as the carrier of truth. Researchers may be partial to a particular framework and its corresponding explanatory concerns but educators must distinguish between beliefs and sentiments *and* accurate empirical assessments. The difference between an educator and a propagandist does not involve a fine or subtle distinction: Educators endeavour to create the conditions for self development while propagandists attempt to determine for others what they should become. Marxism, while not necessarily linked to indoctrination, appears at times to lean in that direction. It behooves the educator who values the Marxist explanatory framework to put eduction first and Marxism second.

Conclusion

In this chapter I have not described and justified a model Marxist educational program, nor have I approached the ethical issues through analyzing a model program since it appears that a single Marxist educational program does not exist. If a feasible Marxist justificatory procedure is as I have described it, distinct social and political settings require distinct educational programs. And so I turn my attention to the characteristic features of a Marxist approach to justification. There are additional reasons for this focus, and these should be emphasized. While they condemn capitalism and offer programs, those within the Marxist tradition have avoided justifying their educational alternatives. Without secure justifications it is reasonable to wonder if the proposed educational solution is any better than the existing system. Another reason for examining the probable rationale underlying a Marxist justification is that the procedure, the non-utilitarian consequentialist approach, is unique among approaches presented in the literature and appears to match one way we assess and justify our actions. As a procedure, however, it is not without problems. Those working in the tradition must begin to examine these problems, especially the issues of extreme instrumentalism and indoctrination. It is time for these difficult and thorny issues to be raised and addressed in the educational literature. Perhaps the justificatory procedure outlined in this chapter will facilitate both the construction and justification of alternative educational programs, programs that will be morally superior to our existing system of education.

7
Explanatory projects and ethical values

In this work I have addressed two central sets of questions: 1) What does it mean to assess Marxist functional explanations of schooling and how does one go about it? and 2) What are the moral values and beliefs embedded in the Marxist tradition and how do these values inform radical criticisms and prescriptions? A third question still remains: How should these moral values affect the Marxist explanatory project? In this concluding chapter I will summarize my responses to the first two questions and identify a few related issues, and then I will address the third and final question.

Marxism, schools, and explanation

While Marxists utilize explanatory modes other than that of the functional form, they tend to rely on and confound various types of functional analysis. Although Marxist theorists criticize "functionalist" approaches, they nevertheless analyze schools' functions and do so without adequate empirical warrant. These functional analyses are problematic. A proper functional explanation (but neither functional attribution nor facile functional explanation) constitutes a structurally sound and empirically examinable explanatory form, but functional explanations cannot account for a specific type of conflict (contradiction) and can be supplanted by intentional explanations. These limitations restrict the use of functional explanation. Still, there is a conceptual and methodological avenue whereby Apple's functional thesis of curriculum selection can be empirically assessed, and the persistence of a connection between curricula and capital is best explained through a combination of intentional and function filter mechanisms. In brief, the Marxist approach to schools has the capacity to offer powerful and empirically examinable explanations of schooling.

My arguments concerning explanation and evidence have presumed a particular intellectual terrain. I have emphasized explanation not interpretation as a goal of social inquiry, and I have accepted as a part of this explanatory telos the search for causal relationships. I think it is appropriate to discuss why this emphasis on explanation and causal investigations does not preclude or undermine the potential value of a more interpretive approach. I will also discuss briefly my belief that the value and vitality of this (and any other) social inquiry depends on a community of reasonable, supportive, but also skeptical individuals. Whether or not such a community exists or can be encouraged to grow is certainly not an inconsequential concern and ought to be addressed.

Throughout roughly the first half of this work, in focusing on the explanatory endeavour in Marxist studies of schools, I have maintained that Marxist explanations ought to be logically coherent and empirically assessable. In Chapter 1, I stated my belief that there are multiple routes for social inquiry. Explanation is not the sole goal of social investigations—a point that needs to be reemphasized. Few educational researchers seem to be willing to accept a pluralist approach within social inquiry; most tend to argue for either an empirical-scientific orientation concerned with observable regularities or social structure or a hermeneutic-interpretive approach focused on meaning. This search for a single method seems misdirected. Instead, we ought to encourage a plurality of logically coherent and empirically examinable approaches. Given the nature of Marxist functional claims, I have not discussed the more interpretive tradition. However, I do not wish to convey, as a result of my chosen emphasis, that educational investigations should overlook this type of inquiry. Much depends on the type of claim advanced. If it is a question of cultural meaning or personal significance, then an interpretive approach would seem appropriate. If it is a question of how the structures of institutions facilitate or inhibit particular outcomes, then causal analysis would seem more appropriate. While investigative issues are never quite so clearly dichotomous, in social investigations the method should fit the central questions, and the range of questions should not be arbitrarily curtailed. Both questions of meaning and questions of structure are concerns that can guide social inquiry, and in educational studies both concerns are important. Still, if radical researchers are going to offer non-functional explanations then these alternative approaches must be internally coherent and empirically assessable. If they are going to offer interpretive case studies their empirical accuracy and theoretical cogency need to be examined.

I have tried to inform further Marxist studies of schooling by analyzing the coherency and empirical accuracy of their claims. My efforts, however, will have value only if they are in turn examined and assessed by a community of researchers. The success or failure of this endeavour is best decided by researchers who share a commitment to rational cannons and an understanding of the Marxist conceptual and value orientation. Although strong divisions exist among radical factions, an associated community (admittedly fragile) of radical American researchers exists. Despite my criticisms of their explanatory framework, Samuel Bowles and Herbert Gintis[1] have offered a seminal empirical study of schooling and capitalism, as has David Livingstone in his research.[2] The historical studies of Jean Anyon, David Hogan, Robert Lowe and William Reese provide further empirical and conceptual refinements,[3] while the theoretical elaborations of Michael Apple, Landon Beyer, Nicholaus Burbules, Dennis Carlson, Martin Carnoy, Walter Feinberg, Henry Giroux, Patti Lather, Henry Levin, Peter McLaren, Philip Wexler, and George Wood continue to furnish formulations worthy of further inspection.[4] This intellectual community need not exclude and in fact should encourage the participation of skeptics who are not committed to the radical framework. At times the radical passion can be blinding. Sympathetic skeptics can help to point out the blind spots. In the last five years Michael Dale, Jeannie Oakes, Michael Olneck, and Francis Schrag have contributed to the radical debate.[5] I do not think any of these individuals would identify themselves as committed radicals but each appears to have an understanding of radical scholarship, and all are committed to rational canons. It is this sort of community, one that includes both individuals committed to the radical framework and also those skeptical but understanding of it, that needs to be encouraged.

Both these committed and skeptical researchers seem to recognize that the radical tradition has the potential to offer valuable explanations that might otherwise go unformulated. This potential seems reason enough to support, nurture, and prod this intellectual tradition. One way to enhance the strength of the radical approach is to offer critical but supportive commentary on its development. In large part the value of my critique of the radical framework will be determined by this community's deliberation.

Marxism, schools, and ethics

Marxists also morally criticize schooling in capitalist societies. In Chapter 5, I maintained that although the standard for these criticisms frequently appears to be one of justice, Marx viewed (and a consistent Marxist tradition would construe) justice as a deficient moral standard. Marx morally criticized capitalism but his standard was freedom (not justice), a standard embedded within a naturalist ethic. Although this standard of freedom provides a basis for the critique of capitalism, it alone cannot provide a justificatory schema for radical educational programs. In Chapter 6, I maintained that Richard Miller's non-utilitarian consequentialist procedure provides a coherent and plausible justificatory approach, one that meshes with the Marxist framework. The Marxist value of freedom, in tandem with this consequentialist procedure, orients the radical tradition toward particular educational concerns but does not prescribe a single or specific educational agenda. Prominent among these educational concerns are curricula enabling a clear and accurate understanding of our social and political world. Finally, I argued that intrinsic to the Marxist ethical framework is a tendency towards indoctrination and moral instrumentalism, tendencies that need to be checked.

Further discussion and analysis should focus on this proclivity towards instrumentalism and indoctrination. In his *Marxism and Morality* Steven Lukes argues well that those working in the Marxist tradition must confront the instrumentalist inclinations of "communism in practice."[6] I agree with Lukes, and in this work I have highlighted the need to inspect these instrumentalist tendencies. Furthermore, a careful reading of George Counts's

Dare the Schools Build a New Social Order? and the work of Paulo Freire demonstrates that the radical tradition has not adequately distinguished education from indoctrination.[7] The instrumentalist and indoctrinatory leanings of the radical tradition cannot go unexamined, especially when one realizes the radical emphasis on democratic educational strategies. While radicals talk of democratic pedagogy and democratic schools and claim that schools should be "experiments in democracy" and teachers should engage students in democratic dialogue,[8] the obvious tension between the democratic vision and the instrumentalist and indoctrinatory tendencies cannot be ignored.

In addition to these tensions there is the conflict inherent in the Marxist focus on both individual freedom and community. In Chapter 5, I related Brenkert's definition of Marxist freedom as the achievement of self determination through the identification and concrete realization of desires, capacities, and talents, with communal relations being a necessary condition for the full realization of individual freedom. What this sort of formulation ignores are the very real antagonisms between individual self determination and communal relations, a perennial problem in human relations and ethical analysis. An ethical examination of Marxist educational agendas should look seriously at this issue. One central difficulty is arriving at a notion of a public (educational) good capable of integrating competing and antagonistic individual goods. Recently, in the educational literature John White has attempted to bridge this divide with his "enlarged conception of self," and Nel Noddings has emphasized an ethic of care as one route to solving this problem.[9] More generally, Alasdair MacIntyre has argued for viewing particular practices (e.g., education) as peculiarly *social* and as entailing the "social" virtues of justice, honesty, and courage.[10] Undoubtedly, other avenues are available. For the educator committed to a democratic socialist future, these possibilities need to be explored.

Marxism, values, and explanation

While I have examined directly the explanatory and ethical adequacy of Marxist explanations, I have not explicitly addressed how the value for freedom should affect the Marxist explanatory project. In Chapter 1, I argued minimally for the goal of impartiality when assessing explanations. Here I wish to extend and elaborate that point. As I outlined in Chapter 5, the Marxist naturalist ethic maintains that human beings are such that in order to be human they must be free. Marx concluded that capitalism unduly restricted humanity's freedom, and for that reason he criticized capitalism. At least two basic normative positions can be derived from these propositions: If in order to be human, people must be free, then Marxists value freedom, and furthermore, if capitalism unnecessarily restricts people's freedom, then Marxists devalue capitalism. Marxist educators, it seems, would value these normative positions and would orient their explanatory studies toward uncovering just how the characteristic features and practices of the public school, its curricula, and capitalism unnecessarily limit the freedom of its employed and enrolled population. As the issue stands now, a Marxist most probably would not be motivated to explain how demographic changes affect public school curricula, what makes principals effective leaders in curriculum development, or how contending status groups affect the development of school subjects. That is, they would not explore these questions unless such concerns could be linked, through capitalism, to a restriction of individuals' freedom.

It seems that such inquiry would be opposed by those who argue that personal and social values ought not enter into our choice of explanatory frameworks. According to this position, the goal of research is to reduce the role of all social and personal values in the scientific endeavour. Here the Marxist concern with freedom would be viewed as either distorting the understanding of educational institutions or as an unhealthy preoccupation restricting investigations and therefore limiting an examination of schools and society. Such claims have been made. And yet it appears inordinately unreasonable to maintain that the role of normative appraisals should be expunged. In order to decide which questions to ask and what to investigate, criteria are necessary, and these criteria are always connected to a set of cognitive and moral values. For example, curriculum studies include investigations of the role of teachers in implementing curricula, the introduction and transformation of school subjects, the cognitive and affective development of children, the bureaucratic and political regulations governing curriculum production and selection, and many other diverse concerns. In each of these areas decisions are made, at some point, regarding what to investigate, what to explain, and what theoretical framework to use to study the area under investigation. Directing an investigation to examine whether curricula, in conjunction with capitalism, restricts individuals' freedom does not seem that much different from examining whether a particular curriculum enhances children's cognitive development. Both the Marxist and the cognitive orientations initially suppose that certain factors affect students' development and then apply the conceptual framework most suited to investigating their respective questions. Without initial beliefs or hunches about the way the world works, we would not have any explanations, much less explanations focused on schooling and curricula.

Although it appears reasonable to expect values to affect the direction and focus of explanations, it seems highly suspect to allow these values to influence an assessment of the accuracy of these explanations. Marxists may believe that schools and their curricula unduly restrict the freedom of the schooling population, but it would be unwarranted to allow these beliefs to intrude in an assessment of whether schools actually do restrict freedom. At times, unfortunately, Marxist explanations have appeared to be determined more by the researcher's beliefs than by the empirical world, but this tendency need not be characteristic of Marxist explanations.[11] I am not assuming that the ever elusive "state of objectivity" will permeate Marxist approaches to schools. I am suggesting that a rigorous assessment of explanatory claims is in order and can be accomplished in a manner such that a Marxist and a skeptic could, in principle, agree about their assessments of the validity of asserted causal claims. Exactly how this can be accomplished is a difficult but not intractable methodological problem, as I have argued in Chapters 1, 3, and 4. There is, however, a need for separating normative appraisals from judgments about the accuracy of such claims.

In Marxist analyses discussion about the validity of explanatory prepositions is confounded by the belief that "validity" is not limited to a theory's cognitive claims but is also a measure of its ability to engage people in meaningful action. As I noted in Chapter 1, a concern for the empirical accuracy of causal claims is either derided as "positivist" or overshadowed by demands for pragmatic or emancipatory tests of a theory. Yet, although he does not disregard the emancipatory "test of validity," Raymond Geuss argues against the strict emancipatory "test" and states that if a "critical theory is to be cognitive and give us knowledge, it must be the kind of thing that can be true or false and we would like to know under what conditions it would be falsified and under what conditions confirmed."[12] He adds,

> . . . critical theories are acceptable if they are empirically accurate and if their "objects," the agents to whom they are addressed, would freely agree to them. A critical theory addressed to the proletariat is confirmed, if its description of the objective situation of the proletariat in society is confirmed by normal observational means, and if the members of the proletariat freely assent to the theory, in particular to the views about freedom and coercion expressed in the theory.[13]

It is evident from Geuss's analysis that the "validity" of a critical theory may depend on more than the empirical accuracy of its causal claims, but it is also clear that an empirical assessment is a necessary (though not sufficient) condition for the acceptance or rejection of a theory.

Given that a Marxist explanation makes knowledge claims about the world and as such requires empirical assessment, the question remains whether the Marxist value for freedom and the belief that capitalism restricts that freedom should affect such empirical assessments. I cannot foresee any plausible argument supporting the view that these Marxist tenets should play a role in the empirical assessment of explanatory claims. To maintain otherwise would be to enter into a solipsistic and relativistic world where whatever researchers assert, they confirm. This would certainly be a sad state of affairs, one that would leave any hope for emancipation dashed on the rocks of cognitive despair.

Radical researchers have a moral obligation as members of a community of inquirers to insure that this state of cognitive despair does not commence. While I have argued that one's beliefs should not affect assessments of a theory's accuracy (and that in this sense values should not affect an assessment of the "facts"), there are certainly ways in which "fact" and value intermingle.

Besides the role of values in guiding researchers towards particular concerns and questions, values affect inquiry in another manner. The radical researcher is morally obligated to produce accurate and trustworthy theories of schooling. Earlier I discussed the role of a community of inquirers in assessing the value of radical scholarship, and I have maintained throughout this work that one criterion in this assessment must be the accuracy of the proposed claims. Now it seems that in order for a community of inquirers to exist as a community of inquirers, in order for individual members to trust the findings of their peers, it is essential that their epistemic claims be accurate and trustworthy. Without honoring the standards of empirical accuracy, the radical community's status as a community of inquirers would be undermined.

Conclusion

There are, to be sure, numerous other issues and complications that arise when a consideration of Marxist normative beliefs, explanatory investigations, and educational prescriptions is broached. I have chosen to examine those issues that I believe are particularly prominent, and I have criticized the Marxist analysis of schooling. This criticism has not dampened by own nor have I intended to dampen others' interest in the radical project. The Marxist analysis of schooling still seems an eminently reasonable, feasible, and morally defensible approach. In many ways much of the spirit of my critique could have been directed towards other educational research traditions, and the standards I have used could and should be applied to other frameworks. I chose the Marxist framework because it seems to me one of the most valuable ones available. My admiration for the work of theorists like Bowles and Gintis, Apple, and Carnoy and Levin is high. Someone who senses that oppression by class, through schooling, is a prominent feature of capitalist societies need go no further than the radical-Marxist tradition. That does not mean, however, that there are not weaknesses in that tradition. There are many. Others may discard frameworks once weaknesses are pointed out. However, I do not think those weaknesses justify discarding the radical tradition. The radical framework's current strengths include its concern for freedom, its theoretical elaborations, and its critique of other traditions. Future efforts will show how well those writing in the tradition can support their explanatory and descriptive claims and add further justification to their moral assessments and practical prescriptions. Without enhanced explanatory claims or moral justification it does not seem likely that the radical tradition will convince reasonable skeptics. I hope it does. Without convincing these skeptics it will inevitably fail. I hope it does not.

Notes

Series editor's introduction

1   Robert Heilbroner, *The Nature and Logic of Capitalism* (New York: Norton, 1985, p. 85.

2   Ibid., p. 53.

3   Adam Smith, *The Wealth of Nations* (Oxford: Clarendon Press, 1976), pp. 709–10.

4   The list of people and publications here would be extensive. For synthetic treatments, see Michael W. Apple, *Education and Power* (New York: Routledge and Kegan Paul, ARK edition, 1985), Henry Giroux, *Theory and Resistance in Education* (South Hadley: Bergin and Garvey, 1983), and Geoff Whitty, *Sociology and School Knowledge* (New York: Methuen, 1985).

5   For a review of much of this work, see Cameron McCarthy and Michael W. Apple, "Race, Class, and Gender in Educational Research," *Race, Class, and Gender in Education*, ed. Lois Weis, (New York: State University of New York Press, 1988).

6   Herbert Gintis, "Communication and Politics," *Socialist Review* 10 (March-June, 1980), pp. 189–232.

7   Andrew Levine, *Arguing for Socialism* (New York: Routledge and Kegan Paul, 1984).

8   Samuel Bowles and Herbert Gintis, *Democracy and Capitalism* (New York: Basic Books, 1986), p. 3.

9   For a discussion of the common good, see Marcus Raskin, *The Common Good* (New York: Routledge and Kegan Paul, 1986).

10 Bowles and Gintis, *Democracy and Capitalism*, p. 5.

11 Michael W. Apple, *Teachers and Texts: A Political Economy of Class and Gender Relations in Education* (New York: Routledge and Kegan Paul, 1986).

12 Ibid.

13 Ibid.

Preface

1   In this work I use the term researcher to refer generally to those individuals involved in disciplined inquiry.

2   Throughout I use the terms "Marxist" and "radical" interchangeably. My rationale for this usage is outlined in Chapter 1.

1 Studying schools and assessing theories

1   Charles Beard, Letter to George Counts, dated August 5, 1934. From the personal files of Raymond Callahan, Washington University, St. Louis.

2   For the origins of this nomenclature and noted examples see Karen J. Winkler, "Flourishing Research in Marxist Theory Belies Signs of Its Demise, Scholars Say," *The Chronicle of Higher Education* 32:19 (1986): 4–7; and Erik Olin Wright, *Classes* (London: Verso, 1985), p. 2.

3   For representative works see Louis Althusser, *Lenin and Philosophy* (New York: Monthly Review Press, 1971); G. A. Cohen, *Karl Marx's Theory of History: A Defence* (Princeton: Princeton University Press, 1978); Antonio Gramsci, *Prison Notebooks* (New York: International Publishers, 1971); Jurgen Habermas, *Theory and Practice* (Boston: Beacon Press, 1973); E. P. Thompson, *The Poverty of Theory and Other Essays* (New York: Monthly Review Press, 1978); and Erik Olin Wright, *Class, Crisis and the State* (London: Verso, 1979).

4   For representative works see Michael Apple, *Education and Power* (Boston: Routledge and Kegan Paul, 1982); Jean Anyon, "Elemen-

tary Schooling and Distinctions of Social Class," *Interchange* 12:2–3 (1981): 118–32; Samuel Bowles and Herbert Gintis, *Schooling in Capitalist America* (New York: Basic Books, 1976); Martin Carnoy and Henry Levin, *Schooling and Work in the Democratic State* (Stanford: Stanford University Press, 1985); Robert Everhart, *Reading, Writing and Resistance* (Boston: Routledge and Kegan Paul, 1983); Henry Giroux, *Theory and Resistance in Education* (South Hadley, Massachusetts: Bergin and Garvey, 1983); David Hogan, *Class and Reform* (Philadelphia: University of Pennsylvania Press, 1985); David Livingstone, *Class Ideologies and Educational Futures* (New York: Falmer Press, 1983); Philip Wexler, "Structure, text and subject: a critical sociology of school knowledge," in *Cultural and Economic Reproduction in Education,* ed. Michael Apple (Boston): Routledge and Kegan Paul, 1982), pp. 275–303; and Paul Willis, *Learning to Labor: How working class kids get working class jobs* (Westmead, England: Gower Publishing Co., 1980).

5   Marxism has long been known for dividing the world up into workers and capitalists. Recent Marxist research recognizes the empirical inaccuracy of this division but maintains the centrality of class structure and class relations. For two examples, see Wright, *Classes*, and Pat Walker, ed., *Between Labor and Capital* (Boston: South End Press, 1979).

6   See D. J. O'Connor, "The Nature of Educational Theory" and P. H. Hirst, "The Nature of Educational Theory, Reply to D. J. O'Connor" in *Proceedings of the Philosophy of Education Society of Great Britain*, Philosophy of Education Society of Great Britain, 6 (January 1972): 97–117; and P. H. Hirst, "Educational Theory" in *Educational Theory and Its Foundational Disciplines* ed. P. H. Hirst (London: Routledge an Kegan Paul, 1983), pp. 3–29.

7   D. C. Phillips, "After the Wake: Postpositivistic Educational Thought," *Educational Researcher* 12:5 (1983): 4–12.

8   Eliot Eisner, "Anastasia Might Still Be Alive, But the Monarchy is Dead," *Educational Researcher* 12:5 (1983): 13–14, 23–24.

9   Jonas Soltis, "On the Nature of Educational Research," *Educational Researcher* 13:10 (1984): 9.

10   This is admittedly an extreme position and, as such, not embraced by all Marxist researchers. It does, however, capture an essential radical reaction to "normal" academic research.

11   Henry Giroux, *Ideology, Culture and the Process of Schooling* (Philadelphia: Temple University Press, 1981), pp. 43–44.

12   Ibid., pp. 44.

13   Ibid.

14   Explicitly Marxist concepts have been used before in United States debates over schooling. For example, see Zalmen Slesinger, *Education and the Class Struggle* (New York, J. J. Little and Ives Co., 1937). The recent use of Marxist concepts owes a great deal to Bowles and Gintis' work, *Schooling in Capitalist America*.

15   Bowles and Gintis, *Schooling in Capitalist America*.

16   Michael Apple, *Ideology and Curriculum* (Boston: Routledge and Kegan Paul, 1979).

17   Anyon, "Elementary Schooling and Distinctions of Social Class."

18   Giroux, *Theory and Resistance in Education*.

19   Carnoy and Levin, *Schooling and Work in the Democratic State*.

20   Frederick Crews, "In the Big House of Theory," *The New York Review of Books* 33:9 (1986): 37.

21   Ibid.

22   Ibid.

23   Jurgen Habermas, *Knowledge and Human Interest*, (Boston: Beacon Press, 1971) p. 4.

24   Richard Bernstein, *The Restructuring of Social and Political Theory*, (Philadelphia: The University of Pennsylvania Press, 1976), p. 193.

25   Ibid., p. 194.

26   Peter Berger and Thomas Luckmann, *The Social Construction of Reality* (New York: Doubleday and Co., 1967) and Max Weber, *The Methodology of the Social Sciences* (New York: Free Press, 1949).

27   Habermas, *Knowledge and Human Interests*, p. 309.

28   Ibid., p. 310.

29   This is the inference many draw. It may or may not be a correct interpretation of Habermas.

30   Raymond Geuss, *The Idea of a Critical Theory* (New York: Cambridge University Press, 1981), p. 75.

31   Ibid., p. 76.

32   Ibid., p. 79.

33   Ibid.

34   Michael Carter, "Contradiction and Correspondence: Analysis of the Relation of Schooling to Work" in *The Limits of Educational Reform*, eds. Martin Carnoy and Henry Levin (New York: Longman, 1976), p. 78.

35   Wright, *Class, Crisis and the State*, Ch. 1.

36   Ibid.

37   Steven Lukes, "The Underdetermination of Theory by Data" in *Proceedings of Aristotelian Society*, suppl. vol. 3 (1978): 98.

38   Bertell Ollman, *Alienation* (New York: Cambridge University Press, 1971), p. 46.

39   See also, Rom Harré, "Philosophical aspects of the macro-micro problem" in *Advances in Social Theory and Methodology*, eds. K. Knorr-Cetina and A. V. Cicourrel (Boston: Routledge and Kegan Paul, 1981), pp. 139–60. Readers should note that I am reacting to a strong materialist position. Many Marxists would not claim that beliefs are determined by class position.

40   Israel Scheffler, *Science and Subjectivity* (Indianapolis: Bobbs-Merrill Co., 1967), p. 2.

41   Ibid., p. 4.

42   Ira Katznelson and Margaret Weir, *Schooling for All: Class, Race and the Decline of the Democratic Ideal* (New York: Basic Books, 1985), p. 8.

43   Ibid.

44   Ibid., p. 25.

45   Ibid., p. 86.

46   Ibid., p. 93.

47   Paul E. Peterson, *The Politics of School Reform 1870–1940* (Chicago: University of Chicago Press, 1985), p. 5.

48   Ibid., p. 22.

49   Ibid., p. 53.

50   Scheffler, *Science and Subjectivity*, p. 13.

51   Ibid., p. 40.

52   Ibid., p. 39.

53   Paul Roth, *Meaning and Methods in the Social Sciences: The Case Of Methodological Pluralism* (Ithica, New York: Cornell University Press, 1987).

54   See Louis Althusser, "Ideology and Ideological State Apparatuses" in *Lenin and Philosophy*, pp. 127–86; and Thompson, *The Poverty of Theory and Other Essays*.

55   Alan Garfinkel, *Forms of Explanation* (New Haven: Yale University Press, 1981), p. 23.

2 Theoretical debates and explanatory claims

1   Alan Garfinkel, *Forms of Explanation* (New Haven: Yale University Press, 1981), p. vii.

2   For similar interpretations see G. A. Cohen, *Karl Marx's Theory of History: A Defence* (Princeton: Princeton University Press, 1978), pp. 283-84; Jon Elster, "Marxism, Functionalism and Game Theory," *Theory and Society* 11 (1982): 453–82; Piotr Sztompka, *System and Function: Towards a Theory of Society* (New York: Academic Press, 1974), ch. 4; and Jonathan Turner and Alexandra Maryanski, *Functionalism* (Menlo Park, California: The Benjamin/Cummings Publishing Company, 1979).

3   Cohen, *Karl Marx's Theory of History*, pp. 283–84.

4   Ibid., p. 249.

5   *Science 84* 5:3 (1984); 6.

6   Samuel Bowles and Herbert Gintis, *Schooling in Capitalist America* (New York: Basic Books, 1976), pp. 234–35.

7   Ibid., p. 159, p. 186.

8   Ibid., p. 157.

9   Ibid., p. 131.

10 Ibid., p. 133.

11 Ibid., p. 147.

12 Ibid.

13 Ibid., p. 235.

14 Herbert Gintis and Samuel Bowles, "Contradiction and Reproduction in Educational Theory," in *Schooling, Ideology and the Curriculum*, eds. Len Barton, Roland Meighan, and Stephen Walker (Sussex, England: Falmer Press, 1980), p. 55. Although Gintis and Bowles express dissatisfaction with their previous work, they still support the empirical accuracy of their correspondence explanation in later works. See Samuel Bowles and Herbert Gintis, "The Crisis of Liberal Democratic Capitalism: The Case of the United States," *Politics and Society* 11:1 (1982): 51–93.

15 Bowles and Gintis, "The Crisis of Liberal Democratic Capitalism," pp. 55.

16 Ibid.

17   Gintis and Bowles, "Contradiction and Reproduction in Educational Theory," p. 55.

18   Ibid.

19   Ibid.

20   Ibid., p. 56.

21   Ibid.

22   Ibid.

23   Ibid., p. 57.

24   Ibid.

25   Michael Apple and Lois Weiss, "Ideology and Practice in Schooling: A Political and Conceptual Introduction," in *Ideology and Practice in Schooling*, eds. Michael Apple and Lois Weiss (Philadelphia: Temple University Press, 1983), p. 7.

26   Michael Apple, "Reproduction and Contradiction in Education: Introduction," in *Cultural and Economic Reproduction in Education: Essays on Class, Ideology and the State* (London: Routledge and Kegan Paul, 1982), p. 11.

27   Apple and Weiss, "Ideology and Practice in Schooling," p. 4.

28   Michael Apple, "Analyzing Determinations: Understanding and Evaluating the Production of Social Outcomes in Schools," *Curriculum Inquiry* 19:1 (1980): 62–63.

29   Apple and Weiss, "Ideology and Practice in Schooling," p. 21.

30   Apple, "Analyzing Determinations," p. 58.

31   Michael Apple, *Education and Power* (London: Routledge and Kegan Paul, 1982), p. 14.

32   Apple, "Analyzing Determinations," p. 59.

33   Apple and Weiss, "Ideology and Practice in Schooling," pp. 20–21.

34   Ibid., p. 25.

35   Bowles and Gintis, *Schooling in Capitalist America*, p. 130.

36   Ibid.

37   This is not to say that people could not organize and struggle for democratic work relations. The point is that, generally speaking, democratically organized and liberating jobs do not exist and therefore are not among peoples' available choices.

38   Apple and Weiss, "Ideology and Practice in Schooling," p. 7. Apple's project to "understand" schools through citing their functions could be interpreted as functional attribution and not

facile functional explanation. If this were the case they would be offering a description, not an explanation, of school's effects. While others disagree, I am convinced that Apple cites schools' functions to explain schools. In Chapter 4 I analyze Apple's claim that a selective tradition characterizes curriculum selection, an assertion that obviously follows a facile form. Other examples of this explanatory approach are available in Apple's work. For instance in his more recent criticism of Mortimer Adler's *Paideia Proposal* (New York: Collier Books, 1982) Apple states:

> In essence, I want to claim that what we are witnessing in schools is not easily fixable, and certainly not by a return to the academy. It is in fact "naturally" generated out of our modes of production, distribution and consumption.
> All too briefly in an economy that needs to stimulate individual consumption and a search for happiness based on the pursuit of consumable goods and services, older cultural values involving respect and the public good *need to be subverted*. Traditional cultural forms are not progressive for capital and need to be replaced by ideologies of individualism. Respect for position and "sacred" culture will be subverted and replaced by respect for possessions. ("Old Humanists and New Curricula: Politics and Culture in *The Paideia Proposal*," *Curriculum Inquiry* 15:1 [1985]: 100).

I do not think any other interpretation of this particular passage would be accurate. Apple explains schooling phenomena ("What we are witnessing in schools") by referring to the needs and requirements of a capitalist economy. What occurs in schools is "naturally" generated out of our modes of production, distribution, and consumption. Schools have functions, and these functions are required by capitalism. As I argued earlier, such an approach is facile; it assumes what requires examination.

39 Ibid., p. 7.

40 Ivan Soll, *An Introduction to Hegel's Metaphysics* (Chicago: The University of Chicago Press, 1969), p. 139.

41 Henry Giroux, "Theories of Reproduction and Resistance in the New Sociology of Education: A Critical Analysis," *Harvard Educational Review*, 53:3 (1983): 261.

42 Ibid., p. 274.

43 Ibid., p. 275.

44 Henry Giroux, "Hegemony, Resistance, and the Paradox of Educational Reform," *Interchange* 12:2–3 (1981): 6.

45 Ibid., p. 11.

46 Ibid., p. 7.

47 Giroux, "Theories of Reproduction and Resistance," p. 259.

48 Ibid., pp. 288–90.

49 Ibid.

50 Ibid., p. 281.

51 Henry Giroux, *Ideology, Culture and the Process of Schooling* (Philadelphia: Temple University Press, 1981), p. 98.

52 See Martin Carnoy, *Education as Cultural Imperialism* (New York: McKay, 1974) and Martin Carnoy and Henry Levin, *The Limits of Educational Reform* (New York: McKay, 1976).

53 Martin Carnoy and Henry Levin, *Schooling and Work in the Democratic State* (Stanford: Stanford University Press, 1985), p. 4.

54 Ibid., p. 19.

55 Ibid., p. 21.

56 Ibid., p. 22.

57 Ibid., p. 3.

58 Ibid., p. 27.

59 Ibid., pp. 96–97.

60 Ibid., pp. 142.

61 Philip Wexler, "Movement, Class and Education," *Race, Class and Education*, eds.Len Barton and Stephen Walker (London: Croom Helm, 1983), p. 23.

62 There are certainly differences among these three authors but their similarities will be emphasised.

63 David Hogan, "Education and Class Formation: The Peculiarities of the Americans," in *Cultural and Economic Reproduction*, ed. Michael Apple (London: Routledge and Kegan Paul, 1982), pp. 47–48.

64 Paul Willis, "Cultural Production and Theories of Reproduction," in *Race, Class and Education*, eds. Len Barton and Stephen Walker (London: Croom Helm, 1983), p. 115.

65 Wexler, "Movement, Class and Education," p. 20.

66 Ibid., p. 22.

67 Hogan, "Education and Class Formation," p. 52.

68   Willis, "Cultural Production and Theories of Reproduction," p. 126.

69   Hogan, "Education and Class Formation," p. 78.

70   Ira Katznelson and Margaret Weir, *Schooling for All* (New York: Basic Books, 1985), p. 224.

71   Ibid.

72   Imre Lakatos, *The Methodology of Scientific Research Programmes* (New York: Cambridge University Press, 1980).

3 The logic and assessment of functional explanations

1   For an analysis of the philosophical issues raised by teleological explanations see Larry Wright, *Teleological Explanations: An Etiological Analysis of Goals and Functions* (Berkeley: University of California Press, 1976), and Andrew Woodfield, *Teleology* (London: Cambridge University Press, 1976).

2   When I speak of laws, positivist or realist, I am referring to generalizations that identify regularities among social events, human practices, and institutional features. These are not universal, timeless, or context-independent regularities. Instead, they presume a general social context.

3   See Henry Giroux, "Toward a Critical Theory of Education: Beyond a Marxism with Guarantees—A response to Daniel Liston" *Educational Theory* 35:3 (1985): 313–20.

4   The realist position in the philosophy of science is outlined by Roy Bhaskar, *A Realist Theory of Science* (New Jersey: Humanities Press, 1978) and Rom Harré, *The Principles of Scientific Thinking* (Chicago: University of Chicago Press, 1970). The implications of this position for the social sciences can be found in Ted Benton, *Philosophical Foundations of Three Sociologies* (London: Routledge and Kegan Paul, 1977); Roy Bhaskar, *The Possibility of Naturalism: A Philosophical Critique of the Contemporary Human Sciences* (New Jersey: Humanities Press, 1979); Rom Harré and Paul F. Secord, *The Explanation of Social Behavior* (Oxford: Basil Blackwell, 1972); and Russell Keat and John Urry, *Social Theory as Science* (London: Routledge and Kegan Paul, 1975).

5   I take this account from Keat and Urry, *Social Theory as Science*.

6   Functional explanations come in various forms and strengths. Here I shall be interpreting functional explanation as an explanation of

the persistence of an event (social or institutional feature). A much stronger interpretation, and one not supported here, is that a functional explanation explains not only the persistence of an event but also the origin of the event. In this chapter I will speak of functional explanations as explanations of the persistence, not origin, of a particular institutional or social feature or human practice. In addition to the persistence/origin distinction there are two possible reasons for a feature's persistence: An institutional feature could have the consequence of minimally stabilizing a situation or providing some sort of maximum benefit (i.e., enhancing the growth of the productive forces in the Cohen-Marx Thesis of Functional Compatibility). Here I will employ both enterpretations but not commit myself to either. I sense that the minimal reading is a more defensible position. For an elaboration see Philippe Van Parijs, *Evolutionary Explanation in the Social Sciences* (London: Tavistock, 1981), ch. 6, 7.

7   G. A. Cohen, *Karl Marx's Theory of History: A Defence* (Princeton: Princeton University Press, 1978), p. 269.

8   Piotr Sztompka, *System and Function: Towards a Theory of Society* (New York: Academic Press, 1974), p. 65.

9   Ibid., p. 67.

10   While I would reject the claim that functional explanations must be reducible to the individual level, this is not to reject the need for a micro-foundation for functional explanations.

11   Cohen, *Karl Marx's Theory of History*, ch. 6, 7.

12   See Erik Olin Wright, *Class, Crisis and the State* (London: Verso, 1979), ch. 3.

13   Here I will follow Cohen and simplify the account of ordinary causal statements for the purpose of the analogy.

14   Cohen, *Karl Marx's Theory of History*, p. 261.

15   Ibid., p. 261.

16   Ibid., p. 261.

17   Ibid., pp. 261–62.

18   Ibid., p. 262 (emphasis added).

19   Ibid., p. 264.

20   Again, I will follow Cohen and simplify the procedures for analogical purposes.

21   Cohen, *Karl Marx's Theory of History*, p. 265.

22   Ibid.

23   Ibid., p. 266.

24   Ibid., p. 269.

25   Ibid.

26   See Jon Elster, "Marxism, Functionalism, and Game Theory," *Theory and Society* 11:4 (1982): 453–82; Anthony Giddens, "Commentary on the Debate," *Theory and Society* 11:4 (1982): 527–39; and Philippe Van Parijs, "Functionalist Marxism Rehabilitated: A Comment on Elster," *Theory and Society* 11:4 (1982): 497–511.

27   Van Parijs, "Functionalist Marxism Rehabilitated," p. 510.

28   Ibid., p. 499.

29   Ibid.

30   In these three examples I will use ability grouping and tracking as synonymous terms.

31   This restriction on functional explanation is entailed by Van Parijs' reinforcement theory of social selection. As noted earlier, Van Parijs' theory assumes a criterion of satisfaction rather than survival in the selection process. In periods of intense conflict competing standards of satisfaction exist. In order for a functional explanation of the reinforcement sort to apply, either the standards must be compatible, or, if incompatible, it must be assumed that the power is distributed unevenly in order to favor one class over another. If neither of these conditions are met—if class conflict entails incompatible standards of satisfaction and undermines a stable and unequal distribution of power—then functional explanations that utilize a theory of reinforcement are unable to explain the outcome. While this restriction surely does not invalidate Marxist functional explanations, it does limit further their explanatory scope.

4 Is there a selective tradition?

1   For examples, see Jean Anyon, "Ideology and United States History Textbooks," *Harvard Educational Review* 49:3 (August 1979): 36–86, and "Elementary Schooling and Distinctions of Social Class," *Interchange* 12:2–3 (1981): 118–32; Michael Apple, *Ideology and Curriculum* (London: Routledge and Kegan Paul, 1979), "Curricular Form and the Logic of Technical Control," in *Cultural and Economic Reproduction in Education*, ed. Michael Apple (London: Routledge and Kegan Paul, 1982, and *Education and Power* (London: Routledge and Kegan Paul, 1982); Frances Fitzgerald, *America Revised* (Boston: Atlantic-Little Brown Books, 1979); and

Joel Taxel, "Justice and Cultural Conflicts: Racism, Sexism and Instructional Materials," *Interchange* 9:1 (1978/79): 56–84, and "The Outsiders of the American Revolution: The Selective Tradition in Children's Fiction," *Interchange* 12:2–3 (1981): 206–29.

2 See Peter Bachrach and Morton Baratz, *Power and Poverty* (Oxford: Oxford University Press, 1970), and "Reply to Merelman," *American Political Science Review* 62:4 (1968): 1268–69; R. M. Merelman, "On the Neo-Elitist Critique of Community Power," *American Political Science Review* 62:4 (1968): 1268–69; R. M. *The Capitalist State* (New York: New York University Press, 1982); and Claus Offe, "Structural Problems of the Capitalist State: Class Rule and the Political System. On the Selectiveness of Political Institutions," in *German Political Studies*, vol. 1, ed. Von Beyme (Beverley Hills: Sage Publications, 1974).

In the political science debate over community power and decision making and in the theories of the state the methodological issues surrounding the notion of a nonevent are discussed. Generally speaking, the notion of a nonevent refers to items that have been excluded from a decision-making agenda. Theorists of an empiricist leaning claim that there are unsurmountable obstacles to an empirical investigation of nonevents. Bachrach and Baratz and Offe have attempted to formulate conceptual frameworks and methodological stances to support analyses of nonevents.

The concept of a nonevent can lead one to suppose an ontologically nonexistent entity. This is misleading. In this analysis the nonevent dilemma (the investigation of curricular topics that are excluded) must be seen in relation to the claims of dysfunctionality in an asserted functional relationship. Curricular topics that are dysfunctional to capital are said to be excluded due to the functional relationship between schools and capital. The concept of a nonevent does not indicate curricular topics that don't exist but rather topics that have been excluded from a curricular "agenda." Here the concern is with constructing a methodological approach that can identify excluded topics and link them to the logic of capitalism. While the Marxist literature contains arguments about both positive and negative selection, the assertions of the selective tradition focus on negative selection. Therefore, I will focus on curricular topics that have been excluded. I think that a methodological and conceptual format similar to the one presented in the following pages could be constructed for claims of positive selection.

3 Bachrach and Baratz, *Power and Poverty*.

4 Offe, "Structural Problems of the Capitalist State."

5   Here I use functional assertions to refer to either functional attribution or facile functional explanation. See Chapter 2.

6   In this chapter the term "causal connection" refers to either a functional or intentional relation.

7   Apple, *Ideology and Curriculum*, p. 19.

8   Ibid., p. 17.

9   Ibid., p. 8.

10   Ibid., p. 102.

11   Apple, *Education and Power*, and Michael Apple and Lois Weiss, "Ideology and Practice in Schooling: A Political and Conceptual Introduction," in *Ideology and Practice in Schooling*, eds. Michael Apple and Lois Weiss (Philadelphia: Temple University Press, 1983).

12   In "Elementary Schooling and Social Class" Anyon states that she wants to identify the reproductive effects of schooling along the lines of "social class." However, in her analysis, and in most other radical curricular analyses, class remains an obscure and underdeveloped concept. The notion of class lacks not only crucial conceptual substance, but its empirical basis is not adequately addressed. While the debates over class are numerous and complex, a definitive account of class and class structure is crucial for any substantial analysis. In this chapter I will not directly confront these issues. However, for the prescriptions outlined in the following pages to be honored, the notion of class will have to be constructed more fully.

13   Taxel, "Justice and Cultural Conflict" and "The Outsiders of the American Revolution."

14   Fitzgerald, *America Revised*. Fitzgerald does not utilize Marxist categories.

15   The difference between this definition and the previous one is that a more broadly causal, rather than strictly functional, relationship is posited.

16   See Roger Dale, "Education and the Capitalist State," in *Culture and Economic Reproduction in Education*; Martin Carnoy, "Education, Economy and the State," in *Culture and Economic Reproduction in Education*; and Martin Carnoy and Henry Levin, *Schooling and Work in the Democratic State* (Stanford: Stanford University Press, 1985).

17   Dale, "Education and the Capitalist State," p. 129.

18   That is, Offe does not assume the strong theses of functionalism as outlined in Chapter 2.

19   Offe, "Structural Problems of the Capitalist State," p. 45.

20   Apple, "Curricular Form and the Logic of Technical Control," p. 248.

21   Sheila Harty, *Hucksters in the Classroom: A Review of Industry Propaganda in the Schools* (Washington, D.C.: Center for the Study of Responsive Law, 1979).

22   Fitzgerald, *America Revised*, p. 175. For accounts of this process, see Alexander S. Rippa, "The Textbook Controversy and the Free Enterprise Campaign," *History of Education Journal* 9:3 (1958): pp. 49–58; and Harold Rugg, *That Men May Understand* (New York: Doubleday, Doran and Co., 1941).

23   Fitzgerald, *America Revised*.

24   For various accounts of textbook publishing, see Hillel Black, *American Schoolbooks* (New York: William, Morrow, 1967); Paul Goldstein, *Changing the American Schoolbooks* (Lexington, Mass.: D. C. Heath, 1979); Thomas Lawler, *Seventy Years of Textbook Publishing—A History of Ginn and Company* (Boston: Ginn, 1938); and James Reid, *An Adventure in Textbooks* (New York: R. R. Bowker, 1969).

25   Apple, "Curricular Form and the Logic of Technical Control."

26   Offe, "Structural Problems of the Capitalist State," p. 36.

27   A dual-class analysis is used for conceptual clarity and simplicity. Surely a discussion of the "middle," "new middle," "professional," or "contradictory" class role in schools is crucial. And, given the assertions of the capitalist nature of public school curricula, any triclass analysis would need to investigate the role of this third class in maintaining both accumulation and legitimation.

28   Offe, "Structural Problems of the Capitalist State," p. 39.

29   See Goran Therborn, *The Ideology of Power and the Power of Ideology* (London: Verso, 1980).

30   Offe, "Structural Problems of the Capitalist State," p. 40.

31   See Meredith Damien Gall, *Handbook for Evaluating and Selecting Curriculum Material* (Boston: Allyn and Bacon, 1981).

32   A principal in the Madison, Wisconsin, public school system pointed out this trend. As a supervisor of student teachers in the public schools, I have also noted this practice. While it serves to clarify the level of procedural selection, this example should not be taken as an empirical substantiation of the presence of a procedural filter.

33   Kenneth Teitelbaum points to some examples of this selective mechanism. See Kenneth Teitelbaum, "Schooling for 'Good

Rebels': Socialist Education for Children in the United States 1900–1940" (Ph.D. diss., University of Wisconsin, Madison, 1985).

34   Julia Wrigley, "The Politics of Education in Chicago: Social Conflict in the Public Schools" (Ph.D. diss., University of Wisconsin, Madison, 1977). See also Julia Wrigley, "Class Politics and School Reform in Chicago," in *Classes, Class Conflict and the State*, ed. Maurice Zeitlin (Cambridge, Mass.: Winthrop, 1981) and *Class Politics and Public Schools: Chicago, 1900–1950* (New Brunswick, N. J.:Rutgers University Press, 1982).

35   Wrigley, "Politics of Education in Chicago," p. 120.

36   Further analysis would need to address the following questions: If segments of the curricula are tied to capital, is the capital-curricula connection the dominant force in determining curricular content? Does this relation significantly constrain and limit other forces impinging on the curricula? Are these other influences independent of capital? In short, and to give a practical twist, what changes in public school curricula must await an alteration in the capitalist socioeconomic order?

5 Ethical values and Marxist educational critiques

1   Samuel Bowles and Herbert Gintis, *Schooling in Capitalist America* (New York: Basic Books, 1976), p. 49.

2   Paul Willis, *Learning to Labor* (Westmead, England: Gower Publishing Co., 1980), p. 120.

3   Henry Giroux, *Theory and Resistance in Education: A Pedagogy for the Opposition* (South Hadley, Massachusetts: Bergin and Garvey Publishers, Inc., 1983), p. 19.

4   Michael Apple, *Ideology and Curriculum* (London: Routledge and Kegan Paul, 1979), pp. 11–12.

5   A brief historical account of the issues raised in the debates over Marxism and morality can be found in Kai Nielsen, "Introduction" in *Marx and Morality* eds. Kai Nielsen and Steven Patten (Guelph, Ontario: Canadian Association for Publishing in Philosophy, 1981).

6   These positions represent general arguments. Individual authors may fit into one or more of these categories.

7 See Allen Wood, *Karl Marx* (London: Routledge and Kegan Paul, 1981) and "The Marxian Critique of Justice" and "Marx on Right and Justice, a Reply to Husami," in *Marx, Justice and History*, eds. Marshall Cohen, Thomas Nagel, and Thomas Scanlon (Princeton: Princeton University Press, 1980).

8 Karl Marx as quoted in Wood, "The Marxian Critique of Justice," p. 14.

9 Wood, "The Marxian Critique of Justice," p. 24.

10 Ibid., pp. 15–16.

11 Wood, *Karl Marx*, p. 143.

12 Ibid.

13 Wood's conception of functional explanation is problematic. He appears to employ a strong paradigm of functionalism in tandem with the "facile" form of functional explanation. See Chapter 2.

14 Wood, *Karl Marx*, pp. 143–44.

15 Ibid., p. 127.

16 Among recent Marxist exegetes John McMurtry, George Brenkert, and Norman Geras view Marx as valuing self actualization and freedom as moral goods. See John McMurtry, *The Structure of Marx's World-View* (Princeton: Princeton University Press, 1978), George Brenkert, *Marx's Ethics of Freedom* (London: Routledge and Kegan Paul, 1983), and Norman Geras, *Marx and Human Nature* (London: Verso, 1983).

17 Wood, *Karl Marx*, p. 126.

18 Ibid.

19 Wood, "The Marxian Critique of Justice," pp. 30–31.

20 Wood, *Karl Marx*, p. 151.

21 Ibid., p. 153.

22 Ibid., p. 154.

23 Ibid., p. 143.

24 Ibid.

25 When Wood argues that for Marx morality is ideological, he includes a third relevant characteristic. In addition to the charge that morality is idealist and functional, he says it is also false. I will not—in fact need not—consider this aspect of falsity. Wood maintains that a person holds a false belief when that individual is unaware of the functional significance of that belief. Since not all moral beliefs need be functional, then a person holding a moral

belief could not be "unaware" of its functional significance—the belief would have no functional effects. If a belief has no function effects for the social system, the individual holding that belief cannot be said to be "holding on" to a false belief.

26   The second principle states:

> After provisions are made for common social (community) values, for capital overhead to preserve the society's productive capacity, allowances are made for differing unmanipulated needs and preferences, and due weight is given to the just entitlements of individuals, the income and wealth (the common stock of means) is to be so divided that each person will have a right to an equal share. The necessary burdens requisite to enhance human well-being are also to be equally shared, subject, of course, to limitations by differing abilities and differing situations (natural environment not class position). (Kai Nielsen, "Capitalism, Socialism and Justice," in *And Justice For All*, ed., Tom Regan and Donald VanDeVeer [Totowa, New Jersey: Rowman and Littlefield]; p. 278)

27   Ibid.

28   For an interesting criticism of a democratic socialist position on economic democracy and fruitful responses see Gerald Doppelt, "Conflicting Social Paradigms of Human Freedom and the Problem of Justification," *Inquiry* 27:1 (1984): 51–86; Carol Gould, "Self-development and Self-management: A Response to Doppelt," *Inquiry* 27:1 (1984): 87–103; and Mihailo Markovic, "Human Freedom from a Democratic Socialist Point of View: A Reply to Doppelt," *Inquiry* 27:1 (1984): 105–15.

29   Martin Carnoy and Derek Shearer, *Economy Democracy: The Challenge of the 1980s* (White Plains, N.Y.: M. E. Sharpe, 1980). Shearer and Carnoy's program has been criticized as "reformist." Whether or not their program would achieve economic democracy is not my present concern. Here I am maintaining that Shearer and Carnoy's program loosely honors Nielsen's principle of economic justice and does not imply an exclusively idealist route for social change.

30   For a criticism of Wood's reading of justice as a relation of correspondence see Richard Miller, *Analyzing Marx: Morality, Power and History*, (Princeton: Princeton University Press, 1984), pp. 78–96.

31   Allen Buchanan, *Marx and Justice: The Radical Critique of Liberalism* (Totowa, New Jersey: Rowman and Allanheld, 1982), pp. 50–51.

32 Ibid., p. 51.

33 To be fair it should be noted that there is disagreement on this point. For a representative sampling see Nancy Holstrom, "Exploitation," *Canadian Journal of Philosophy* 7:2 (1977): 353–69; Gary Young, "Justice and Capitalist Production: Marx and Bourgeois Ideology," *Canadian Journal of Philosophy* 8:3 (1978): 421–55; and Ziyad Husami, "Marx on Distributive Justice," *Philosophy and Public Affairs* 8:1 (1978–79): 27–64.

34 Karl Marx as quoted in Richard Miller, *Analyzing Marx*, p. 28.

35 Miller, *Analyzing Marx*, pp. 29–30.

36 Ibid., p. 24.

37 Geras, *Marx and Human Nature*, p. 101.

38 Holstrom, "Exploitation," p. 359.

39 Brenkert, *Marx's Ethics of Freedom*, p. 17.

40 Ibid., p. 88.

41 Ibid.

42 Ibid.

43 Ibid., p. 93.

44 There is a striking similarity between Marx's notion of freedom and Dewey's conception of growth. In "Dewey's Conception of Growth" (an unpublished manuscript) Daniel Pekarsky has analyzed Dewey's criteria for growth in a manner that could prove helpful for a Marxist analysis of freedom.

45 Brenkert, *Marx's Ethics of Freedom*, p. 101.

46 Both Richard Bernstein and Nicholas Lobkowicz discuss Marx's notion of praxis and transformative labor. See Richard Bernstein, *Praxis and Action* (Philadelphia: University of Pennsylvania Press, 1971) and Nicholas Lobkowicz, *Theory and Practice: History of a Concept from Aristotle to Marx* (South Bend, Indiana: University of Notre Dame Press, 1967).

47 Brenkert, *Marx's Ethics of Freedom*, p. 112.

48 Ibid., p. 125.

6 Ethical values and Marxist educational prescriptions

1 Henry Giroux argues in this way. For a representative sample

see Henry Giroux, "Theories of Reproduction and Resistance in the New Sociology of Education: A Critical Analysis," *Harvard Educational Review* 53:3 (1983): 257–93 and *Theory and Resistance in Education: A Pedagogy for the Opposition* (South Hadley, Massachusetts: Bergin and Garvey Publishers, Inc., 1983).

2 For examples in the Marxist analysis of schools see Michael Apple, *Education and Power* (London: Routledge and Kegan Paul, 1982); *Education and the State Vol. 1 Schooling and the National Interest*, eds. Roger Dale, Geoff Esland, Ross Fergusson, and Madeleine MacDonald (Sussex, England: Falmer Press, 1981); and Martin Carnoy and Henry M. Levin, *Schooling and Work in the Democratic State* (Stanford: Stanford University Press, 1985).

3 George Counts, *Dare the School Build a New Social Order?* (Carbondale, Illinois: Southern Illinois University Press, 1978); Herbert Kohl, *36 Children* (New York: The New American Library, 1967); and Jonathan Kozol, *Free Schools* (Boston: Houghton Mifflin, 1972).

4 Robin Small notes this in his forthcoming work, *Marx and Education*, ch. 3.

5 Ibid.

6 Generally one separates as distinct and independent activities the justification and the construction of educational programs. Within the radical project these two endeavours go hand in hand. A justified educational program should be a feasible program, one that has a chance of being implemented. A realistic assessment of a program's potential for implementation should be a part of the program's justification. Justification without realistic appraisal has a tendency to create idealist formulations.

7 Michael Apple discusses briefly the need for a conception of justice to the "left" of John Rawls's theory. See Michael Apple, *Ideology and Curriculum* (London: Routledge and Kegan Paul, 1979). See also Chapter 5 of this work.

8 Henry Giroux, "Hegemony, Resistance, and the Paradox of Educational Reform," *Interchange* 12: 2–3 (1981): 3–26.

9 At the beginning of this chapter I argue that if schools contribute to the transformation of capitalism, then it is reasonable to construct educational programs for social change. If Giroux is arguing this point, I agree. He seems, however, to be making a stronger claim: If the world changes dialectically, then radical pedagogies are justified. On this latter point, I disagree.

10 Jean Anyon, "Elementary Schooling and Distinctions of Social Class," *Interchange* 12: 2–3 (1981): 126.

11 Ibid., p. 127.

12 Eugene Kamenka, *The Ethical Foundations of Marxism* (London: Routledge and Kegan Paul, 1962) and *Marxism and Ethics* (London: Macmillan, 1969).

13 Derek Allen, "The Utilitarianism of Marx and Engels," *American Philosophical Quarterly* 10:3 (1973): 189–200; "Is Marxism a Philosophy," *Journal of Philosophy* 71:17 (1974): 601–12; and "Reply to Brenkert's 'Marx and Utilitarianism,' " *Canadian Journal of Philosophy* 6:3 (1976): 517–34.

14 Richard Miller, "Marx and Aristotle: A Kind of Consequentialism," in *Marx and Morality*, ed. Kai Nielsen and Steven Patten (Guelph, Ontario: Canadian Association for Publishing Philosophy, 1981) and *Analyzing Marx: Morality, Power and History* (Princeton: Princeton University Press, 1984). The reader should note that I am using Miller's analyses to portray Marx's *ethical* procedure of justification. Miller would not agree with my characterization of Marx's logic of justification as an *ethical* procedure. Miller joins Wood in this respect, arguing explicitly that Marx presents an "anti-morality" point of view. I do not think Miller's position is defensible and will, for the remainder of this chapter, assume that Miller's non-moral characterization of Marx is flawed. However, this difference does not affect how I will portray Miller's description of Marx's logic of justification. We differ in that Miller views it as a humane but non-moral logic of justification while I view it as an ethical justificatory procedure. Miller would, I believe, agree with the mechanics as I present them here.

15 Miller, "Marx and Aristotle," p. 327.

16 For a defense of utilitarian justification of educational activities see Robin Barrow, *Happiness and Schooling* (New York: St. Martin's Press, 1980).

17 Miller, *Analyzing Marx*, pp. 35–41.

18 Miller, "Marx and Aristotle," p. 326.

19 Both Miller and Wood would agree with this list of general goods. Both, however, would characterize them as "nonmoral goods."

20 Miller, *Analyzing Marx*, p. 56.

21 Ibid., p. 76.

22 Paulo Freire, *Cultural Action for Freedom (Cambridge, Massachusetts: Harvard Educational Review and Center for the Study of Development and Social Change, 1970) and Pedagogy of the Oppressed* (New York: Seabury Press, 1974).

23 Anton Makarenko, *The Road to Life* (New York: Oriole Editions, 1973) and *Anton Makarenko: His Life and His Work in Education*, ed. Valentin Kamarin, (Moscow: Progressive Publishers, 1976).

24 Here I am referring to the characteristics of Marx's ethical procedure as outlined by Miller. I am not making any claim about Marxist or socialist political movements. However, with regard to political movements it seems clear that partisans of the left, right, and center have all indulged in extreme and violent forms of political action.

25 Anyon, "Elementary Schooling and Distinctions of Social Class," and Giroux, "Hegemony, Resistance, and the Paradox of Educational Reform."

26 Miller, *Analyzing Marx*, p. 61.

27 Brenkert, *Marx's Ethics of Freedom*, p. 184.

28 Richard Norman, *Reasons for Actions* (Oxford: Basil Blackwell, 1971), p. 94.

29 Here the focus will be on the value of freedom as the predominant value in Marx's catalog of general goods. A problem arises, one that I will not confront, when the consequences of an action relate positively to one good but negatively to another. If the Marxist logic of justification is going to be a viable procedure, conflicts of these sorts must be capable of resolution. With the focus on freedom I have dodged, temporarily, this problem.

30 Brenkert, *Marx's Ethics of Freedom*, p. 88.

31 Stephen Castles and Wibke Wustenberg, *The Education of the Future: An Introduction to the Theory and Practice of Socialist Education* (London: Pluto Press, 1979) and David Reynolds and Michael Sullivan, "Towards a New Socialist Sociology of Education," in *Schooling, Ideology and the Curriculum*, ed. Len Barton, Roland Meighan, and Stephen Walker (Sussex, England: Falmer Press, 1980). Neither of these proposals is conceptually sophisticated, and my summaries are somewhat cursory. However, even with these limitations, their respective views on freedom are evident. Further, both programs are designed as educational proposals in advanced Western capitalist societies. This shared orientation allows the comparison of their views.

32 Castles and Wustenberg, *The Education of the Future*, p. 2.

33   Ibid., p. 33.

34   Ibid., pp. 167–68.

35   Ibid., p. 169.

36   Ibid., p. 181.

37   Ibid., p. 174.

38   Reynolds and Sullivan, "Towards a New Socialist Sociology of Education," p. 185.

39   Ibid., p. 184.

40   Ibid., p. 187.

41   Ibid., p. 188.

42   Brenkert, *Marx's Ethics of Freedom*, p. 116.

43   Ibid., p. 122.

44   Michael Matthews, *The Marxist Theory of Schooling* (Atlantic Highlands, New Jersey: Humanities Press, 1980).

7 Explanatory projects and ethical values

1   Samuel Bowles and Herbert Gintis, *Schooling in Capitalist America* (New York: Basic Books, 1976).

2   David Livingstone, *Class Ideologies and Educational Futures* New York: Falmer Press, 1983).

3   Jean Anyon, "Ideology and United States History Textbooks," *Harvard Educational Review* 49:3 (1979): 36–86; David Hogan, *Class and Reform* (Philadelphia: University of Pennsylvania Press, 1985); David Tyack, Robert Lowe and Elisabeth Hansot, *Public Schools in Hard Times: The Great Depression and Recent Years* (Cambridge, Mass.: Harvard University Press, 1984); and William Reese, *Power and the Promise of School Reform* (Boston: Routledge and Kegan Paul, 1986).

4   This is, of course, not an exhaustive list. For illustrative examples see Michael Apple, *Teachers and Texts* (Boston: Routledge and Kegan Paul, 1987); Landon Beyer and George Wood, "Critical Inquiry and Moral Action in Education," *Educational Theory* 36:1 (1986): 1–14; Nicholaus Burbules, "A Theory of Power in Education," *Educational Theory* 36:2 (1986): 95–144; Dennis Carlson, "Teachers, Class Culture, and the Politics of Schooling," *Interchange* 17:4 (1986): 17–36; Martin Carnoy and Henry Levin, *Schooling and Work in the Democratic State* (Stanford: Stanford University Press, 1985); Walter Feinberg, *Understanding Education* (New York: Cambridge University Press, 1983); Henry Giroux, *Theory and Resistance in Education* (South Hadley, Massachusetts:

Bergin and Garvey, 1983); Patti Lather, "Issues of Validity in Openly Ideological Research: Between a Rock and a Soft Place," *Interchange* 17:4 (1986): 63-84; Peter McLaren, *Schooling as a Ritual Performance* (Boston: Routledge and Kegan Paul, 1986); and Philip Wexler, *Social Analysis of Education* (Boston: Routledge and Kegan Paul, forthcoming).

5   For examples see: Michael Dale, "Stalking a Conceptual Chameleon: Ideology in Marxist Studies of Education," *Educational Theory* 36:3 (1986): 241–58; Jeannie Oakes, *Keeping Track* (New Haven: Yale University Press, 1985); Michael Olneck and David Bills, "What Makes Sammy Run? An Empirical Assessment of the Bowles-Gintis Correspondence Theory," *American Journal of Education* 89:1 (1980): 27–61; and Francis Schrag, "Education and Historical Materialism," *Interchange* 17:3 (1986): 42–52.

6   Steven Lukes, *Marxism and Morality* (New York: Oxford University Press, 1985).

7   These are two exemplary radical works. Neither author seriously examines the indoctrinatory implications of his position. Counts talks about the distinction between education and indoctrination but does not address the indoctrinatory difficulties his work implies. Freire's pedagogy is based squarely on a bi-polar "class" view of the world and assumes an adult population. See George Counts, *Dare the School Build a New Social Order?* (Carbondale, Ill.: Southern Illinois University Press, 1978), and Paulo Freire, *Pedagogy of the Oppressed* (New York: Seabury Press, 1974).

8   See Carnoy and Levin, *Schooling and Work* and George Wood, "Schooling in a Democracy: Transformation or Reproduction?", *Educational Theory* 34:3 (1984): 219–40.

9   John White, *The Aims of Education Restated* (London: Routledge and Kegan Paul, 1982) and Nel Noddings, *Caring A Feminine Approach to Ethics and Moral Education* (Berkeley: University of California Press, 1984).

10   Alasdair MacIntyre, *After Virtue: A Study in Moral Theory* (Notre Dame, Indiana: University of Notre Dame Press, 1984).

11   Andy Hargreaves, "Resistance and Relative Autonomy Theories: Problems of Distortion and Incoherence in Recent Marxist Analyses of Education," *British Journal of Sociology of Education* 3:2 (1982): 107–26.

12   Raymond Geuss, *The Idea of a Critical Theory* (London: Cambridge University Press, 1981), p. 75.

13   Ibid., p. 79.

Index